MY LIFE AS A ROCKET

FROM BUILD TO LAUNCH

COLIN DE SOUZA

Dedicated to Geraldine, my wife, my angel.

FOREWORD

Many years ago, a colleague and I were talking about his impending retirement. He still had eight years before he could retire but was already wondering what to do, what would life be like and how would he survive financially. I listened quietly because these questions could very well apply to anyone. Perhaps, I should be asking them myself as he was only eight years older than I was. Retirement would come quickly for me too.

I asked him what he thought his life span would be, how long he expected to live. He laughed. Assuming he would be in good health, he would want to live like the Ancients from the Old Testament. I pressed him for a number because an idea was forming in my mind. It was a concept I had not thought of or heard before. He laughed again and then realized that I was very serious. "120! Aim high and you'll get to be 100!" he declared.

That was us. That was our grading philosophy. All our examinations had a really high passing grade so you either get an A or you fail. No getting by on Bs, Cs, or Ds. We'd always aim for 100%. Some got that. Others mostly in the 90's. If you aim for 80%, you might get 79%. That would be a failing grade. So, we always aimed high.

I looked at him and said softly, "If you retire at 60 and live to 120. You are only at the halfway mark. What are you going to do for the other half?" He was stunned. That perspective came as a shock. While he stared at me, I went on. "We've always thought of our training period, our apprenticeship, in blocks of 5 years. Then we carried on working until we retired. Some 35, 40, 45 years later. Even though we would always be learning, we never considered training as anything beyond that block of 5 years."

He looked intently at me. He leaned forward and rested his chin on his hands. "What are you saying?" he asked me quietly. I chose my words carefully. "What if our entire working life, our career, is nothing more than one huge apprenticeship. To learn about life, about our work, about our relationships, about finance, about so many things. As many things as we could handle, as many things that could possibly capture our interest, our passion, our strengths, our talents and qualities that we do not even know that we are capable of yet. And all this time, preparing ourselves for when we really start living - after retirement."

He drew in a breath sharply and he sat bolt upright, looked at me with his mouth wide open. "That is unheard of!" He exclaimed. "We go to school, we work, we retire. We die and get out of the way. That is how it has always been. What are you suggesting?" That was the moment when the concept of our life in stages was redefined for me. Like that of a rocket, each stage had a purpose and a mission. Every individual's life plays out in stages. Each stage is different for each person. The duration of each stage differs for each person and what defines a stage will certainly differ from one person to the next. But, first, every rocket has to be built and then transported to the launch pad before it can take off. This book is a story of one such rocket. My rocket. From Build to Launch takes us from the sixties to Launch day.

1

IN THE BEGINNING

Two events had a major effect on my youth. The 1963 murder of President John F. Kennedy and the emergence of the Apollo space program. President Kennedy was killed on November 22. I was almost three years old, but I remember my mother coming home from work and telling my Father about it. She was shocked, saddened and horrified. She conveyed those emotions to my dad and certainly to me. I can still remember her grief-stricken face today as clearly as when she told him. I did not know who he was or what he meant to the country or to the world. It was only as I grew older that I learned more about him and what he had done in the short time he was President. It was his challenge to Americans to be the first to put a man on the moon that resulted in the frenetic activity by the American space agency in the following decade.

As a young child, I was fascinated by the black and white television images of every rocket launch and I soon became attracted to the immense power of the mighty Saturn V Rocket that took the Apollo astronauts into space. I got rocket toys for Christmas. I made models of the Friendship, Gemini and Apollo capsules and that fascination grew into all things that flew. I was drawn to Aviation and wanted to be a pilot. While that longing still remained, I ended up spending my whole life as an Engineer, making sure airplanes were safe to fly. This was how my career came to be. A world event, a fascination, a hobby, a curiosity all led to a passion that has lasted till this day.

The build and final assembly of a rocket takes place in a building that NASA calls the VAB - Vehicle Assembly Building. It is assembled upright on a mobile launcher and later mounted on a crawler - a transporter unit that moves the whole assembly out of the building, then about three miles to the launch pad. This takes almost five hours at a steady, measured pace. It is the slow (almost agonizing) process from assembly and countless testing to the actual three-mile journey to the launch pad that determines a successful rocket launch and shapes the destiny of its flight. A great percentage of a rocket's life is actually spent on the ground.

As soon as I could, I applied to join the National Airline as an Apprentice Aircraft Maintenance Engineer. The selection process was rigorous. After three selection stages, an initial cohort of 700 was whittled down to 120. I was one of those successful candidates. As the five-year program rolled on, this number reduced even more to a final count of 82 at the fourth year. I did not know it then, but this training period would shape my life and my thinking in ways I could never have imagined. With great anticipation, we went through a fairly normal program that seemed to be going like clockwork. Then, during, our fourth year, we were laid off.

2

THE FIRST LESSONS - MINDSET AND MONEY

It was April 1, 1982. We were almost at the end of our fourth year when we were summoned for a meeting. We were told that we and all forms of training programs in the airline were to be shut down in 90 days. We were being laid off and depending on where we were in the program, we would be given a retrenchment benefit. For myself and my buddies, it would be $6,600 each in 1982 dollars.

We came into the program with nothing. Now, after spending four years at the prime of our lives, we were getting kicked out with exactly what we came in with - nothing. I was just months away from being a qualified Engineer and with nothing, I could not even apply for a job elsewhere. I had been dreaming about this since I was in grade school. There had been nothing but a laser focus on completing this training, graduating and becoming an Aircraft Engineer. No social life, no distractions, no parties. Now this announcement came out of the blue and was a complete shock. We were numb. Someone thought it was a cruel April Fool's joke but it was not. We left the meeting in silence.

I saw many of my friends go through the classic Kubler-Ross grief cycle: denial, anger, bargaining, depression and acceptance. I remember going through denial very briefly. Then I went straight to the bargaining phase. It was pointless to get angry. Something had to be done and there was not a moment to lose. I felt very strongly that it was not logical to let go so many of us especially after the airline had made two multimillion-dollar orders for new aircraft. Expansion was on the horizon; oil prices were on the decline and the shortage of engineers within the airline was beginning to be felt as aircraft from the first order began to arrive. But how could I tell a mighty airline it had made a mistake? Virtually impossible and with the human mindset of pride and the philosophy of face saving, made overturning this decision a very serious challenge. I thought about this for weeks since after all, I did have 90 days. I shifted my mindset to finding a solution. This first real lesson would serve me well throughout my life, all the way to launch. The need to find solutions kept coming up over and over again. This mindset of finding solutions became a major part of my mental foundation and conditioning.

Slowly an idea formed. I was beginning to be aware of an unseen language. A language so universal, so powerful, so prevalent in our world but not taught to many. I was still in the bargaining stage, but I wanted to bargain with as much chance of success as I could manage. There would be no second chances. In the normal process of negotiations, one needs to negotiate from a position of strength. I was in no such position. I needed to be successful on my first and only try. I chose to speak in a language that they would understand. The language of money.

Even back then, large corporations were run by accountants and Human Resources. So, I found myself in front of the HR Manager one day to pitch my case. I explained that I was just months away from getting my first qualification and shortly after, my second. With these, I would be able to find a job elsewhere. I proposed that they should use the $6,600 that they had already committed to giving me to continue paying me every fortnight like they were doing now until I had completed my training and graduated with the qualifications that I could use elsewhere. I had calculated that I would have just about covered the period left. If there was a shortfall, I would bear the cost. If there was excess, they could return the unused amount.

I repeatedly stressed that it was a win-win situation. A win for them in that it would be at ZERO cost. Another win for them because I could come back to serve them if they needed someone home grown in the near future. That is not normally how a win-win works but I made it a point not to paint myself into the equation. It was an idea I knew that she could carry successfully up the food chain and naively hoped that both HR and Finance could not find much fault with. That I was essentially offering to work for free might have crossed her mind and possibly registered as a bonus in this mad scheme. Against all odds, the mighty airline amazingly said yes to a trainee.

3

THE NEXT LESSONS - MORALE AND BULLYING

I was quite surprised that not many of my friends were ecstatic with my proposal to the airline. I had also negotiated that this proposal be applied to all my friends but instead, I faced a sea of disbelief and ridicule. They said that the airline did not want us, and we ought to accept that and leave. Only two others agreed to stay but their resolve dissipated. They left after a short time leaving me very much alone. I was not a person to depend on company in my activities. I had already left the safety of numbers once before when I parted ways with my schoolmates and joined the airline while they went on to other things. Now I found myself the only trainee in the airline and everywhere I went, I was met with surprise, mocking and name calling.

Many people thought that I had made a huge mistake. Many people did not see what I saw. They only saw what was. I saw what might be. I saw potential. I saw a life that I had envisioned for so long, just within but yet still beyond my grasp. They saw a lone ranger in a hostile environment. And they urged me to quit. To seek safety. To run while I still could. To take the money. I refused. The name stuck and from then on, I was their "Lone Ranger." Soon that nickname became, "Loner." Some people remember that to this day. It took several months before, grudgingly, they came to respect my decision. They slowly started to accept me into their fold, the older engineers took me under their wings and started to do what is usually done in these situations. Be a mentor. Be a friend. Be a future colleague. But it took some time.

All except one guy who took it upon himself to be my personal tormentor. He would rain abuse on me, call me names, insult my logic, hurt my feelings, embarrass me in public. All day every day. I did nothing. I said nothing. My focus was long term. My vision was unwavering. This menace was just an insect. He was nothing. I stayed silent. But when I was alone, when I was in a weak moment, self-doubt and self-pity crept in. I would be in despair and I would have to fight these internal demons to keep my morale up. To restore my faith in myself, to keep on keeping on, to press on regardless. It took a tremendous amount of energy to repair my morale every evening. It was mentally exhausting. I soon realized that morale is as thin and as fragile as an eggshell. It serves its purpose but when abused, it can easily break. But unlike an eggshell, morale can be repaired-over and over again. But no one should have to do this. One day you just get plain sick and tired and you snap.

I was in the Engineers' room one day using the data bank library when Insect came in. He began to hurl abuse at me as usual. The other engineers looked uncomfortable but did not intervene. I did nothing for a while, but I could feel my blood boiling in a way I had never felt before. Without warning - even to myself - I erupted. I flung back the chair and charged at him. Insect was taken aback and stepped back quickly until he was against the wall. I still charged at him with my face contorted into a snarl. I stopped inches from his face, my fists clenched and my mouth hurling abuse in a torrent that I had never done before. This continued at full volume for perhaps a whole minute before I was spent and needed to catch my breath. I came to my senses and quickly left the room. I was very conscious of the thunderous silence I was leaving behind.

I thought I would get into trouble for yelling at a senior and perhaps lose my job but before I could fully recover, Insect came out of the room and came at me and started hurling abuse at me again! This is that damn philosophy of face saving. Insect had been made to look like a fool in front of others and he thought having a go at me would help him regain his stature. That was a huge mistake. I erupted again and this time more ferociously than before. If I was going to get the sack, I was going to earn it. Now this environment was different. It was the large aircraft hangar and there were dozens of workers around. They were used to this Insect having a go at me. Some even took pity on me. But this time, they saw me chewing his head off, spitting it out, going for his guts and spitting that out too. They stopped and stared and the whole hangar floor became silent as I continued my barrage at him. He backed away under this fresh assault until he reached the safety of the Engineers' room and scampered back inside.

There was a pause and a bit of silence and then the whole

hangar erupted into cheers and claps and wolf whistles. I turned around and saw them, no longer my teachers and seniors but my friends and colleagues. I waved graciously and took a bow. Insect never bothered me again. In fact, he left the company long before I did. And I did not get the sack after all.

4

HAVE COURAGE AND ASK. WHAT COULD YOU LOSE?

The airport I grew up training in was getting too small and congested. Let's call it Old Airport. I was fond of Old Airport. It was in use from the early 1950's but expansion had it limits and the government decided to build a New Airport. I grew up spending a lot of time in Old Airport. I went most weekends and every school holiday. I was there to watch the first B747 land in Old Airport when Pan Am introduced her to our skies. Then came the Concorde and we had two very iconic airplanes we were lucky to have seen on a regular basis. I spent many days watching and listening to these and many other airplanes come and go and pictured myself working amongst them. I literally grew up around Old Airport.

The time came for the handoff from Old Airport to New Airport. New Airport opened on July 1st. Everyone in the country was abuzz in anticipation. There was speculation as to which airline would be the first to land, if there would be glitches, holdups and confusion. There were public tours of new airport to get people familiar with spaces, parking, arrival and departure public areas. There were behind the scenes tours to areas that would be restricted to airport staff and real travelers. There were dry runs and dress rehearsals and existing Airport staff had to be split up to operate both Old and New airports to keep the Old Airport running efficiently while taking turns to learn and be familiar with New Airport. The goal was an instantaneous transfer from one to the other with no hiccups, delays or confusion. Other airports in the world had transitioned from one to another with major problems and New Airport was determined not to be one of them. Everyone was focused on New Airport.

Except me. Old Airport was my stomping ground. I knew and had been to most places except one. The Control Tower remained a mystery. That's where it all happened. We got the airplanes in good working order. Others looked after crew, fuel, food, passengers, cargo, security, immigration, it all came together like a fine orchestra. Air Traffic Control takes the whole assembly and make the airplanes sing. Unlike the visible areas of an airport operation, only a few people interact with Air Traffic Control. They are largely heard but not seen. There is a tower but only pilots and a few others get to interact with them. Once New Airport starts operations, the Old Airport will take on a new role and I would never know or see the inside of this last piece of the puzzle. I had to do something.

On June 29th, I stood at the base of the Tower Building. The control tower itself, with its iconic slanted windows, sat at the edge and on top of an eight-story building. I looked up nervously. I had no business there. This was long before 9/11 and security was not like it is today. As it was after office hours, there were few people about. I rode the elevator to the top and there in front of me was a steel door with the words "Control Tower" on it. I tried the handle and the door opened! I was amazed. Had it been locked I would have simply turned around and went back down. I listened for alarms, running feet, shouts of "who's there!" But there was only silence. I was very nervous and stood there for many minutes, too scared to go forward though I wanted to. Finally, I realized that this was my chance, tomorrow would be too busy as it would be the last day of Old Airport. I was sure others would want to come visit as well. It was now or never. I opened the door expecting shouts to come at any minute.

Instead, I saw a metal spiral staircase. That's all. The cavity was otherwise empty. Of course! The tower was above the building! I closed the door quietly and peered up. The room above was in semi darkness and I could hear murmuring. I stood there at the bottom for several minutes letting my eyes get used to the dim light and listened to the sounds that came from above. I was so nervous I started to sweat. I was half expecting someone to swing open the door at any moment and that there would be shouts and alarms. But nothing happened. I slowly ascended the stairs one step at a time expecting a squeak or a rattle to give me away. I questioned myself at each step, one half of me telling me quietly to go on and the other half of me screaming at me to turn around and run. Step by step I made my way up until my head emerged through the floor level and I looked around. I was like a submarine's periscope stealthily peeking out from the waves. I slowly looked around and saw a few people bent over consoles, some were speaking into microphones, some were just listening, one was standing and peering out with binoculars. I slowly covered the whole room and came face to face with a pair of leather shoes.

I can't be sure, but I must have peed a little for I knew instantly that there were legs in those shoes. I looked up in horror and saw a man peering down at me. Before I could say anything, he put his finger to his lips to indicate silence and waved me up. I scampered up those last few steps and came around to where he was. He held out his hand and shook mine firmly. He led me over to a console that was set higher than the others and brought a second highchair and motioned me to sit with him. In low tones he introduced himself as the Tower Supervisor and asked for my story. He relaxed when he learnt I was just an inquisitive apprentice after a bit of nostalgia and seeking a private historical moment.

Over the next three hours, he told to me how it all worked. How each controller manned a sector, how they divided their duties looking after housekeeping maintenance traffic, airplanes moving on the ground and airplanes coming in for a landing or getting lined up for takeoff. He also explained that there was another set of controllers a little way off from the airport that manned the long-range radar and guided the airplanes away from and into the airport. The Tower controllers would either hand airplanes to or receive airplanes from these long-range radar controllers. It was fascinating. Operating in low light, soft tones, I sat and listened. I soon started to be able to listen to the supervisor and listen to the controllers at the same time. This form of simultaneous stereo hearing was further refined and practiced when I started flying on commercial flights as a positioning engineer. It soon became a multitasking skill where I could follow two conversations at the same time. This superpower freaked the kids out later when I could have a conversation with my wife but listen in on the kids as well.

I have never been in another control tower since that night. Security these days would never allow me even near one. But the lessons it taught me were not forgotten. Be brave. Ask the question. Don't be afraid to fail. Don't be afraid to look silly. What is the worst that could happen? Recognize an opportunity and seize it. Don't make excuses. Don't give up. Hesitate only to evaluate not to increase uncertainty. Be decisive without taking unnecessary risk. And think of the end result and focus on the prize. Always.

5

NO MEANS NO. REALLY?

At one point, Engineering was operating out of both old and new airports. Our new home at the New Airport was not ready and the 747s flew every Sunday from the New Airport to old airport for its maintenance. It was a mere 20 minute flight. Having completed the work in a week, the airplane would be flown back to New Airport with just two pilots and a flight engineer. These back and forth flights went on for many, many months. The day would come when we would see the last of these B747 flights come in, get renewed and leave Old Airport one last time. I started thinking that when that day came, I wanted to be on board that final flight out of Old Airport.

The week of the final B747 check drew near and when it was certain that this was the last one, I asked a senior person this question: "How do I get permission to fly on board this airplane to New Airport this Saturday?" He gave me an incredulous look. Then he said simply, "You can't." "Yeah I know, I'm still a trainee." So, I asked the next senior person and he said there was no such thing. I asked the Foreman and he laughed and asked me who I thought I was.

So that exhausted my immediate chain of command. I then went to the training school and my own training Superintendent. He snorted and asked me this very seriously "If I can't, what makes you think you can?" I thanked him and went to see HIS manager. His answer was the most dismissive. "Impossible!" he barked. I was used to this by now and I asked him calmly if he would mind if I asked the Deputy Director of Engineering? He knew me by now and my tenacity for following up on an idea. He looked at me icily and answered, "Go ahead. But the answer will still be no."

Well I was running out of cards and I had two more people in Engineering to ask before I went to Flight operations to plead my case. I remember this episode very well. I rode the elevator up to the top floor of Corporate HQ over in New Airport, an area of rarified air where mere mortals like us do not tread. The floors were carpeted, there was oak timber everywhere and people walked on puffy clouds of self-importance. I found my way to the office of the Deputy Director of Engineering.

The key to power lies in only one place: The Personal Assistant. Madam Secretary. Just like Gandalf the Grey, she or he alone determines who shall and who shall not pass. As I walked up to Madam Secretary, she was busy filing her nails. She looked up and down at this scruffy waif that was before her and asked in her most bored and disdainful voice, "Who are you and what do you want?" This was rude and was designed to intimidate. I pictured her as another Insect and that immediately settled my nerves. I introduced myself and declared that I wished to see the Director on a personal and urgent matter. She sat bolt upright at my impertinence but before she could say anything, I asked her nicely, "It is important. Can you help me please?"

Before I knew it, I was ushered into his office. The Man's office was a long and deep one with an imposing view of the runway and it took several steps to get across it. The Man stood up from his desk, a warm smile on his fatherly face, walked around to greet me halfway across with his right hand outstretched. We shook hands and he offered me a seat on the sofa. He was curious to know me, asked me all kinds of questions, took an interest in what I did, what I had hopes for and how I was coming along in the program. After all, I was the Last of the Tribe, the only trainee, the Lone Ranger. From him, I learnt the importance of listening to learn, listening to understand, listening to appreciate. And just like many people in public office, a perfectly normal conversation can be had between strangers by first listening and asking a related question followed by an answer and another related question and before you know it, you will be chatting for hours.

Finally, he asked how he could help me. That was a revelation! Most people would ask what I wanted. He asked how he could help me. The way the question is phrased predisposes the speaker to wanting to find a solution. The mindset is primed into finding a solution and that was a light bulb moment for me. How you phrase a question or a sentence, sets the stage for a desirable or undesirable outcome. The difference being your attitude. He wanted to help me. He wanted a satisfactory solution. For the first time in this quest, I had hope.

I told him what my plan was, my lack of progress in finding a solution going up the food chain and that was how I ended up in his office. I explained what it meant to me, a symbolic act that would complete my work in Old Airport and begin a new chapter in New Airport. He listened intently and simply replied, "Why not?"

Another light bulb moment. People say no because they think it's no or because saying yes means work for them. (I'll just let that sink in for a minute) They let their own self-limiting beliefs stop themselves from achieving more and by extension, no one else would be able to succeed as well. In this case, I had reached the one person whose position allowed him to see things from a different perspective than the rest of the muggles and whose attitude of finding solutions made him want to make this succeed.

I told no one of the arrangements. Nor did I tell them I was in possession of something none of us knew existed - a Flight Deck Pass. On the Saturday morning of the last flight out, I quietly showed the Flight Deck Pass to my Foreman. He read it and reread it and he looked at me and smiled. He patted me on the shoulder and said quietly, "You did it. Have fun, good luck." We remain friends to this day.

All of us were taking photos around the airplane, everything was ready when the flight crew arrived. The Captain greeted us and thanked us for looking after the airplane and then looked around and asked, "Who's Colin?" I stepped forward and he warmly shook my hand and said "Welcome! Let's go!" I grinned from ear to ear and bounded up the stairs after them. At the top, I turned back to view a sea of stunned faces and open mouths. I waved once and disappeared into the aircraft. That was the first time I had been in the flight deck of a B747 actually taxiing under its own power. I had moved airplanes before but that was with a towing vehicle. This was an actual flight with real pilots and a flight engineer and I was there amongst them, the four of us in an otherwise empty airplane. Predict the future by creating it! This was evidence that visualization is a very effective empowering tool and reverse engineering a vision into a series of actionable steps makes it all come to pass. Little did I know that in the course of the next 30 years, I would be in the flight deck of several different models of airplanes as I flew as a positioning engineer. I enjoyed that flight immensely. It was fun. It was symbolic. It was a mere 20 minutes. I saw Old Airport for the last time and have never been back since. But it taught me heaps. No doesn't always mean no. Not in my book. Not since. Not ever.

6

LEAVING THE VAB - ONE LAST
CHALLENGE

I had been on my own for three months when I was awarded my first qualification - A License to maintain and certify the engine of the B747. I was over the moon! I was beginning to realize the dream of one day becoming an engineer. This license officially made me one. The event made me understand and experience once again, the meaning of the phrase "The only way to predict the future is to create it." This was only the beginning. It was, however, insufficient to get me a job as these credentials are best served in pairs. In my case, being a mechanical engineer, I needed the other half of the equation - the Airframe or the mechanical bits of the B747. I continued to plug away at my craft and experience was coming in fast and furious. I was lapping it up and I inched my way towards that second goal. Then it happened. Another event that would change my life, how I looked at things and the realization of how insignificant we all really are.

In September 1983, an accident happened with one of our airplanes. It cost $7 million in 1983 dollars and would take almost three months to repair. That would be worth about $18 million today. I was involved along with three others. I was still a trainee with just a few short months to completion. In a matter of seconds, an uneventful evening turned into a nightmare that would keep me up for nights on end, sick with worry and that feeling again of being alone and abandoned. How could I possibly keep my job this time? I was so close. The airline was massively short of staff and I thought I had a great chance of staying on after I was fully ready.

The airline had of course to mount an investigation and a technical inquiry. If the findings showed that there were grounds of negligence or some form of wrongdoing, the next step would be a disciplinary inquiry. To our surprise and consternation, the proceedings bypassed the technical aspect and went straight into a disciplinary inquiry.

The three other people involved were represented by their respective Unions. I was a trainee. No one represented me. Suddenly I was invisible. Everyone wished me well from a distance. I had to conduct my own defense. I was 22 years old. What did I know about conducting my own defense? I went through all the physical evidence that all of us had in order to prepare. I had the manuals, the company procedures, the physical parts of the failed unit and everything we needed to prove very clearly that a pre-existing fault that was hidden in a non-standard tool the company had bought, caused this accident. I went over everything in detail, repeatedly testing myself, did my own examination and tried as much as I could to pre-empt possible lines of questioning. I went over and over the minutes leading up to this accident and was very sure we had followed all the procedures.

The day came and I was the first one to be called in. I was surprised. Surely, they would have wanted to speak to the others first. At the end of the day, when they had run out of time, they would run through me quickly and it would be over. I went in and saw about 20 people seated all around the room. People of high rank that I knew of but never met. Sitting in the front of the room were the three members of the Disciplinary committee. One was from HR, one from Finance (huh?) and one from Flight operations.

The first question came from Finance. "Do you know how much YOUR accident cost us?" What?! I thought we were here to find out what happened? Then it hit me like a freight train. This was no inquiry. This was a witch hunt. They wanted scapegoats. They must have realized that there was physical evidence to show that their equipment was defective and that maybe the insurance company would not pay for the damages if they found out. Oh, my goodness. This changed everything. I became super guarded after that and made sure all my answers were clear, consistent and unwavering. I was questioned in turn by each member of the committee, the most persistent was the chap from Flight operations. At every twist and turn, he would try to catch me out and make me stumble. He made offensive and accusatory allegations to rattle me and hoped I would stutter and contradict myself. He was the most persistent in putting forward theories of how the accident happened and I had to counter each allegation with physical evidence and flight deck system observations to disprove his theories. I spent almost all of the two hours doing nothing but deliver rebuttal after rebuttal. Finally, it was over, and I was let out.

I was shaking from both the physicality of this ordeal and from the anger at the direction this inquiry had taken. I was livid with the injustice of this blatant bullying attack that they did not even bother to disguise. All they were looking for was a means to put forth their pre-determined findings and the truth and facts took such a back seat they were practically out the door. I was mentally exhausted and I left. I was not allowed to mingle with the others who were held in a separate room. I did not know for how long they were questioned or what had transpired at each. I just had a very bad feeling.

It did not take long for them to deliver their verdict. As predicted, they determined the accident was caused by a combination of events that truly was laughable if it wasn't so devastating to us. Without going into detail, imagine someone telling you in all seriousness that a six-car pile-up on the highway was caused by the front car suddenly going into reverse at 100 miles an hour while being invisible. The insurance company accepted their findings and the airline did not fork out a cent. The other three were punished severely. I was let off with no explanation. I presumed it was because I was a trainee and therefore was not culpable. I never found out the real reasons. It was bittersweet because despite the huge sigh of relief for myself, I felt despair for the other three. They paid a huge price. This lesson made me realize that we were all digits to them. We did not have feelings. We did not matter. Whatever it took- find and falsify if necessary- the means to justify their end. Money took precedence. Truth was irrelevant.

It was almost time for this rocket to leave the VAB. It felt complete. It felt ready to start making the three-mile hike to the launch pad. Were all my challenges over? I didn't know it yet, but one final stumbling block lay right at the edge of the VAB and it was blocking my path.

7

THE DOORS ARE LOCKED

My training period was coming to an end. I had obtained my second license and was now a qualified 747 Engineer. I knew the arrangement I made with the airline. If they didn't need me, I would have to leave. I was so hopeful, so confident that I would just simply graduate and seamlessly join the engineering department as an engineer. After all, the section I was in was desperately short of staff, a condition that would remain for the next 20 years. Overtime was high. People were constantly asked to come back on their days off to supplement the numbers that did not exist. I rubbed my hands in glee. It was all coming together at last. I had made a huge gamble and it was about to pay off. I had an appointment to see the HR manager to hopefully receive my graduation certificate, transfer and appointment papers. I was in high spirits as I entered her office and sat, looking at her in anticipation.

"So, Mr. de Souza, as per our agreement, your last day will be Tuesday, Feb 28, 1984 and the remainder of the money we have been holding for you, $942 will be paid into your account. Do you have any questions?" I was stunned. Shocked. Still disbelieving what I had just heard, I stammered, "But…but what about the shortage? There is overtime needed every day." "Nope. No shortage. We have sufficient staff" was her response. Forget denial and anger. I went straight into bargaining. "But surely one person would not make a difference? They need more engineers. My Chief Engineer said so. Please!" She looked coldly at me and said, "Look, maybe so. But the rest of the people whom we had let go would write to the press and make us look bad." That face-saving nonsense again! Logic, practicality, cost saving all out the door for fear of losing face in the public eye. "But they had the option to stay just like I had" I said. She stood up and left without another word.

I sat outside her office to think and catch my breath. Her secretary looked at me with sympathy for the door had been left open and she had heard everything. It was January 31st. I had four weeks to think of something. I was out of aces. I had no more cards to play. I needed external help. Just as the Deputy Director of Engineering could come up with a solution for my short flight, perhaps my own Department Manager could help me. I had to try.

I went back to my section and waited to speak to him. Let's call him Boss. Boss listened to my story and was sympathetic. He promised to try and find a solution. I thanked him and left. At 7 am the next morning I was back in the waiting room of Boss's office. This section had Boss, two smaller bosses and their secretaries. There was no one in the office except the cleaners. Soon, the secretaries came in. They knew me and offered me a coffee and a biscuit. Smaller bosses came and smiled. Then Boss came in. He was surprised to see me and I asked if there were any developments. He shook his head and went into his office. I stood up, thanked the Secretaries and left.

I was back again the next morning and the next and the next. It was always the same answer. Nothing. I did this every single weekday morning for three weeks. I was getting a little desperate, more than a little panicky when at three and a half weeks, Boss had nothing. By now, the secretaries were joining me in having the coffee and the biscuit. They and smaller bosses were very sympathetic and encouraging and they urged me to keep up my hopes. This was a real test for my faith and morale. It was coming down to the wire and there was no solution in sight. I kept praying and I focused all my energy on Boss and kept renewing the confidence that he would find an answer. I did not turn to ask any other person, I just focused on Boss. Years later, I learnt this from Robert Kiyosaki: FOCUS = Follow One Course Until Successful.

On Friday, February 24, as usual everyone was there and we were quietly chatting when Boss came bursting into the office. "I've got it! I've got it!" He exclaimed. "Come into the office". There he explained his brainwave. A Technician had retired the day before. What Boss proposed to do was that I take his place. Not as an Engineer but as a Technician. He promised that as soon as he could, he would upgrade me to be an Engineer. Was that acceptable? Hell yeah! A foot in the door is worth two on the street. He asked me to come back on Monday morning because he had to run this by HR first.

Monday morning came and Boss was all smiles. He asked me to go see HR lady again today. Waiting outside her office was nerve wracking but Secretary was all smiles. Apparently, she had heard something encouraging about me. HR lady came and ushered me into her office. "Well! You are one persistent young man!" She said. "Your Boss made me an offer and just as you did to me last year, I could not fault it. But we have our conditions. You still have to leave tomorrow Feb 28th, we will still pay you $942, you will have a break on Feb 29th and rejoin us as a technician on March 1". Oh dear. Was this complication really necessary, I wondered? She must have read my thoughts for she said abruptly, "This is the offer. Take it or leave it." Once again, I was not in a good position to negotiate. I took it.

I will never know what went on in Boss's mind all those days when he had to tell me repeatedly that he had no news for me. He must have felt bad. I don't know if he found a solution because he honestly wanted to help me or was it sheer "fed up-ness" that made him think of a solution. After knowing him a little more in the next few years, I realized he was a good man and that he genuinely was seeking a solution. In any case, it was a win-win but in this win-win, I was part of the equation. I used part of that money to treat my parents and my sister to a fabulous meal. After all this time, this Rocket was finally out of the VAB.

8

BE AN AIR BENDER

I embraced my new job eagerly. The staff already knew me and my story. So, it was an easy transition from being a trainee to a technician. Since I actually had an Engineer's License, the airline had a provision where technicians like myself would rise up the technicians' ranks rapidly. Very quickly, I found myself in a lead role. I worked with all kinds of airplanes and so many different airlines. This exposure was incredibly valuable for me in the world of aviation and I welcomed it and looked forward to these new experiences. Two months into my new job, I met an angel and we started dating. Later in the year, Boss was transferred, and New Boss took over. New Boss knew of my history and kept me up to date with prospects of a promotion. After 18 months in the technicians' ranks, New Boss was happy to promote me to the position of Engineer and I was transferred to a different section.

I added three more aircraft type ratings to my name. After the tumultuous time in the VAB, those formative years looked to be over and things were now settling into some semblance of a normal life. In 1988, angel and I were married. I had a regular job with fixed timings and a routine of sorts. Angel and I started to build our lives together and we made plans and mapped out our hopes and dreams.

One afternoon just before the end of the day, I received word that one of our airplanes was grounded in Honolulu and needed an engine replaced. Would I lead a team up there to do that? By now, I had replaced engines on different airplanes many times but had never done this overseas, so I quickly agreed. After some preparation, 13 of us flew off to Honolulu with the spare engine and other equipment to carry out this task. Once we arrived, we quickly got down to work and eventually, the new engine was up and we were ready to do the final testing.

A newly installed engine of a 747 in that era required a full engine testing procedure to be done before the airplane could be released. Among the dozen or so different tests, a full power test required us to bring the engine up to almost it's take off power setting and take note of the parameters and observe if there were any anomalies. There was no proper place in Honolulu that allowed us to do this safely so the local FAA mechanic, let's call him Mr. Aloha, had to taxi our aircraft using its own engines, to the end of one of the runways. Once there, we would take over and carry out our tests.

Back at our home base, we were used to doing these tests in our facility where we could position the aircraft facing into the wind. The engines of that era were very susceptible to fluctuations of the wind direction and they required any prevailing winds to be coming in from the front. Never from the side or even at an angle. Engines are like racehorses. They are made for motion. While barreling down the runway and into flight, the air is always coming in from the front. But a stationary engine gulping in huge volumes of air, needed the air to be coming in straight at it. Never from the side.

Mr. Aloha had taxied our aircraft to the reef runway 08R. Since we were essentially occupying an active runway of a really busy international airport, doing this at 2 am seemed like a good idea. I took my place in the left seat in the flight deck, Mr. Aloha remained in the right seat in case we were told to get off the runway and my Avionics buddy "Sparky" manned the flight engineer's console. I was dismayed to see from the windsock, that the winds blowing across the runway were at right angles to us, from right to left. It wasn't a breeze; it was a really strong wind. I couldn't possibly run the engines like that. I tuned to Mr. Aloha and asked him when those winds would die down. "Mmmm… April, maybe May". It was November!

I had no choice but to try. No. 3 engine on the right wing was to be tested and I slowly advanced the thrust levers of both No. 3 and No. 1 for balance. As expected, before I could go very far, No. 3 started making rough, angry noises which we refer to as "growling". This was the reaction of the engine when the air coming in the front was turbulent and from an angle. At this stage, if I advanced the thrust levers any further, this new engine would stall and could very well be damaged in the process. I slowly throttled back. I looked at Sparky who slowly shook his head. I turned to Mr. Aloha and asked for any suggestions. He mused a little and said simply, "Create your own wind."

Back in home base, we had choice of direction. We had strict rules of operation. We could not run more than 2 engines at a time. We not only had the aircraft parking brakes on but had many heavy metal wheel chocks placed in front and behind each landing gear. All these were to help prevent the airplane from moving forward when we increased the power. Now here we were in Honolulu at 2 am with all four engines running, no heavy metal wheel chocks and nothing but parking brakes. Stranded passengers were waiting for us in the terminal. We were on a 12,000 foot long runway that was a mere 200 feet wide with the sea water on either side and a cross wind that didn't let me do my job. And Mr. Aloha here wanted me to create wind.

He was serious. I thought for a moment and nodded. I turned to Sparky and said, "Get ready!" I had all the lights on, I placed my left hand on the steering tiller, my feet braced against the brake pedals in case we moved and with my right hand, gripped all four thrust levers and pushed. Slowly advancing them forward, I felt the airplane straining, wanting to move forward. I hesitated. I was afraid. I was in no man's land. No one could have possibly done this in our airline and I had no terms of reference. I let the airplane and the engines stabilize before I continued advancing the thrust levers slowly forward. The engines started to make little growling noises but soon settled and I continued. I scanned the instruments, the runway, the windsock and kept my ears focused on listening to the engines, alert to any signs of trouble. I kept advancing the power and slowly, almost imperceptibly, I started to see the windsock start to move its tail toward me. I was amazed and elated! I carried on advancing the power and the engines changed from a high pitch whine to a deep, thunderous roar.

I reached the point in the high-power setting that I was aiming for and by then the awesome suction power of four mighty 747 engines influenced the winds and turned their direction in my favor. The windsock had turned ninety degrees and was now indicating a full-on head wind. I was an Air Bender!

Sparky recorded our parameters and I kept three engines at high power while we completed all the other tests on the new No. 3 engine. We finished, handed over control back to Mr. Aloha and taxied back to the terminal. On our way back, I looked at the windsock and it had returned to its original position. Even at this point, I could scarcely believe what we had just done. With the airplane soon back in the air, with its plane load of passengers, we returned to our hotel. I thought about what we had just experienced and realized that it would probably be a once in a lifetime event. I didn't think I would ever do that again and I never have. It all came back to finding solutions. But you need to know the rules in order to break them properly. You don't always have to be the one with the answers. When you are the dumbest guy in the room and you ask the Universe, the Universe will answer. In the face of impossible odds, never give up. It was a lesson I will never forget.

Before we parted, Mr. Aloha confessed that he had only thought about it but had never ever seen it done. I guess we all learnt something that night.

9

BOSS GOES TO DISNEYLAND

Language is used to communicate. From one person to another, ideas, thoughts and wishes flow back and forth. In the business world, methods, procedures, instructions govern the operating systems, company culture and other necessary human interaction. The spoken word or the words we think very often help decide our outcomes and our attitudes play a major role in this. I firmly believe it is far better to say, "What if" instead of "If only". There are many other two-word combinations that are most futile and do nothing to enhance our lives. "Would have", "could have" and "should have" are banned from my thoughts and speech along with "I wish", "I hope". Regret does nothing. If there was a mistake, learn and remember the lesson. Then move on. Just as Mr. Deputy Director asked me, "How can I help you?" asking ourselves or those around us, "Should we" ... or "what can we do?" will greatly change our mindset into thinking before an event, planning for an event and even recover from an event in a way that is constructive and forward thinking and with little time for regret. But there was one, "Should I…?" moment I will never forget.

It was in a meeting with one of the smaller bosses. He had all the group leaders in a conference room and it was a discussion on change and improvement. There were about 15 of us including some note takers and observers. After a lot of debate on the state of affairs in our division, the question was asked, "What can we do to get better?" Many people had suggestions which were debated and either kept for future thought or dismissed. I kept silent and cast my eyes down. Finally, smaller boss singled me out. "Colin, I know you have something to say. What do you think we should do?" I looked around the room and some were shaking their heads as if to tell me to shut up. "I might, but all of you will laugh at me," I said. Of course, that made the whole room laugh. But smaller boss didn't give up. "I know you; you always have thoughts on things like this. Go on, I promise we won't laugh." he said solemnly.

I looked around the room and back again at smaller boss. "You need to go to Disneyland", I said. The whole room erupted with howls of delirious laughter. Everyone was in full roar including smaller boss, the note takers and observers. I had to smile and even chuckle at this amusing sight. Some people were wiping tears from their eyes and many people were starting to wipe their faces and spectacles while still giggling. Finally, smaller boss managed to compose himself and called the room to be silent while still grinning from ear to ear. "Hold on, hold on guys. Let's hear him out. Colin doesn't usually say things like this without good reason."

Almost all of us in that room had been to Disneyland. We worked in the airline and it was simple and free for us to travel to most of the Disney Parks around the world. So, I knew that once I explained myself, people could relate. "The experience starts the moment you arrive," I explained. "How do you cope with that massive influx of people and vehicles coming into the parking lots and parking structures in a short period of time in the morning? Then moving those people from those locations to the entrance of the park, process them through ticketing and security and have them streaming in to the park and then repeating the process in reverse as they all make their way home when the park closes. They have their peak periods when moving people and vehicles is crucial and has to be done smoothly, in a timely manner, with minimum wait times and zero accidents and all done with a smile. We have our peak periods too. Airplanes come and go in two very furious time slots each day. We ought to learn from them how they manage their staffing levels during peak and nonpeak periods and compare that with how we are currently managing our staffing levels." By now, the room was silent.

I went on about staff training, staff welfare, staff rotation, equipment maintenance and high standards of service quality. I compared each topic with Disney Parks as the reference. Smaller boss looked at me thoughtfully. "Don't reinvent the wheel, is that what you're saying?" I nodded. "Find a mentor. Learn from the best in the business. We are not the first ones with this problem," I said. "Be the dumbest guy in the room."

I constantly look around at my group. The people I mix with, the ones I listen to or read about. If I am the smartest one in that group, I should leave that group. That is a very effective way of constantly improving my exposure and my thinking. The first thing I believe, is to recognize that you do not have the monopoly on ideas. You are obliged to look around and find ways of doing things better, more effectively. It always starts with knowing what is broken and then finding ways to fix it. You may have an idea on what might be done. Look or ask around to see if someone else has done it better or even if you could improve on what someone has done and maybe adapt it to your needs. Complaining about a situation does not correct or improve anything. See something, do something. It could be personal, financial, work related, relationship related or community related. Goal setting comes from recognizing a need or a deficiency in your area of interest and taking small concrete steps to resolve that need or deficiency.

Smaller boss never asked The Mother of all Bosses permission for a working trip to Disneyland. But I bet he never looked at Disneyland the same way ever again.

10

GOAL SETTING AND MOON MISSIONS

So now my Rocket and its entourage of mobile launcher platform and crawler-transporter were well and truly out of the VAB and moving at snail's pace towards the Launch pad. Launch day was somewhere in the distant future. While I was crawling along, I had no idea when launch day would be. It's like moving along a track in the dark not knowing when that track would come to an end. You just kept going.

What about setting goals? I knew what I wanted to do. Launch my rocket. I roughly knew where we would be going. Up there, out there. Apollo 11 knew its mission was to go the moon, put two humans on it briefly and then all crew members would come back. For the purpose of this book, my first mission is to get from build to launch. The reality of life is different. The timelines and stage duration and description is only done retrospectively. Launch day would only be known when that day came. But before that happened, I knew that I was somewhere along that three-mile trek between the VAB and the launch pad.

Getting built was a definitive set of activities. We've already covered the high points. The journey to the launch pad was littered with experiences and events that shaped my path and modified my thinking at every step of the way. If there was some way someone could find a new way of getting things done wrong, that would happen. If there was an important event or activity that required focus and concentration, someone would come up at that exact moment and tap your shoulder about something so insignificant and inconsequential but end in totally derailing your activity. Distraction and preoccupation can sometimes cause you to stop at a green light. Imagine the consequence of that!

Getting from Point A to Point Z has to occur in some form of a sequence. You open the garage door before driving out. So, when we set goals, we first need to identify exactly what we want to achieve. We know we need to launch but right now, when that will be is unknown. But we work our way towards it. We break it down in bite sizes, we make targets that seem possible, we cross check our process and our progress and we make changes on the run because, as you know, life gets in the way.

No matter what the goals and the tasks are, they all come with a requirement to be treated with the respect they deserve. Whether it was a huge financial commitment to buy a home, planning a family vacation, taking a course of study and graduate or to get fit and lose weight, all these goals had to be treated seriously. They needed to be treated as Missions.

As in the Military, missions are treated very seriously. They require the dual accomplishments of successful completion. Let me repeat that. Successful completion. No half and half. No partials, no ifs, buts or maybes. Here is the mission. Get it done.

Every task we undertake, every goal we set, every project we accept has to have the status of a mission. With that mindset, we are mentally set up to succeed. But again, life does get in the way doesn't it? Apollo 13's original mission was to land a third pair of humans on the moon but after they developed a failure in their spacecraft enroute, the mission was changed to that of returning all three members to Earth, alive and well. Stubborn and blind insistence in following a mission in spite of its certain demise is irresponsible and foolhardy. Good and practical leadership requires us to adapt, adjust and, if necessary, change the mission in the wake of undeniable evidence pointing to its impending doom. Changing mission parameters is not on debate here but changing the attitude towards a mission is non-negotiable. Doing what is required always supersedes doing what is desired.

11

IN THE DEPTHS OF DESPAIR

In 1991, Angel and I were sent by the airline to manage one of its overseas destinations. We were there for five and a half years. By the time we came back to our home country, we had Prince and Princess, three years apart. But the time spent there itself was a steep learning curve for Angel and I. We had to learn a different language, understand the people and their beautiful culture, adapt to different food and get used to things that were done in ways that were alien to us. The constant stability of the love and support from Angel was crucial in this new world. The other constants in my life were the airplanes. Airplanes have always been and still are the sweetest creatures that humans have made and I have the privilege to interact with them on a daily basis. They may be late; they may get a little sick and they may tease and tickle you and challenge your skills and knowledge. But they never bite, they never argue, they never cheat or bully or take advantage of you and it is never, ever personal. When humans treat them right and give them the proper care and handling they deserve, they go on for a long time. But, on one occasion, one of my dearest airplanes tested me the way no other airplane has ever tested me.

It was November 11, 1991. We met for the first time. She was a B747 Combi. She carried both passengers and cargo in the main deck. It was a huge effort to put this contract together. There were pilots and flight engineers from one country, flight attendants from another country, owned by one company, leased to another and we looked after Engineering. So, on that day, we met . It was the inaugural flight for her new operators. We were tasked with looking after her in three cities in our adopted country. After that, she would fly internationally to the USA. Turn around and come back the same way. Back and forth along this route, she would do this for the next two years.

We left the home city and flew one hour to the second city. I was onboard as the travelling engineer and looked after her in the second city. After that, we flew again. After three hours, we landed in the third city. Third City had a 12,000 foot runway built during WW2 but this was the first time, Third City had ever seen a B747. The TV cameras were there, the Mayor came out, the Elders came to bless the airplane and there was a lot of fuss and fanfare. This was the last stop in this country and the next sector would be many hours over the ocean to the USA. I was supposed to leave the flight at Third City and wait for her to return two days later and repeat the process. Over the next two years, my colleagues and I took turns being stationed in Third City for a month at a time. But before all that could take place, I had to first dispatch her over the water to the USA. But she refused to go.

A long flight over the ocean required a lot of fuel. Having

filled her wing tanks to capacity, all that remained was the last one, the fuel tank in the center, right between the wings. We had almost reached the target volume of that tank when she sprung a leak. Not a trickle, not a drizzle but a full-on gushing fuel leak. It came from somewhere near the bottom of that tank. When I saw this fuel leak, I was dismayed because I knew this airplane could not make it to the USA. It was a desperate situation. With little or no equipment for a major task like this, the fuel leak continued unabated. There was fuel in the wheel wells and on the tarmac. The pool of fuel kept getting larger and larger. As this was meant to be just a refueling stop, all the passengers and crew were still on board. I informed the flight crew and urged the immediate disembarkation of all persons.

Having emptied the airplane, the only way to stop the leak was to empty the tank. There was almost 50,000 lbs. of fuel in that tank and we had to take that out quickly. Third City was a simple place. The usual flights were domestic in nature, small propeller or light twin jets operated here. There was no large fuel tanker that we could deposit the fuel into, but the Air Force nearby had one. A small one. Its capacity was a mere 5000 lbs. of fuel. It would fill up in no time, make a 45-minute round trip to empty itself and repeat until the fuel leak stopped. It would take about 10 hours. I had to manage the airplane, stay in touch with the flight crew and run to a communications hut in between tanker visits.

Communications in 1991 in this remote outpost is the stuff of legends. Forget the internet. Forget cell phones. Think telex machines with punch hole tape and an encoder-decoder machine. To make a long-distance call to main base, I had to speak to an operator to give him the number and then hang up.

He would then connect from island to island, patch by patch until he got through. Then he would ring me back and connect me up. To get to that stage, took about 45 minutes. This communications hut was about 150 yards from the airplane.

I had a young chap stationed at the comms hut to alert me when a call came through. I would then run, take the call and then hang up. HQ was giving me data and suggestions which I had exhausted and I was giving feedback on the progress. These calls went on throughout the evening, into the night and well into the early morning. I had never run so much for so long ever. All this time the tanker kept coming back to fill up and I would be in the flight deck and select the correct pumps from which to take the fuel from. Then a call would come through and I would run to the comms hut. And then run back for the next tanker fill.

At some point through the night, just as the tanker was about to come back, a call came through. I told the staff there to wait until I came back. After the call, I dashed back only to find that the tanker had filled up and left. I was grateful. That saved some time. Then a thought occurred to me. These people didn't know the airplane. I didn't tell them how it was done or what I was doing. They merely thought I wanted to take fuel out and so take fuel out they did. From the wrong tank! Not only that but they fumbled in the process and caused a lock out of the whole system. I now had an unbalanced airplane and a frozen fuel system that normal resets would not fix and a wasted tanker trip that took fuel from the wrong tank. I shook my head and sat down in disbelief.

The flight crew saw me putting my hands on my head and came over. They had already calculated that they could first fly back to Home City. As time went on, they reached the point where their duty hours only allowed them to fly to Second City. And that deadline was rapidly approaching. Dawn was breaking and I was exhausted. We had been doing this all night. I had no food, no drink, no help and had been awake for almost 24 hours and running back and forth to take and make those phone calls. The passengers and crew were all scattered around this small airport, some even lying under the stars with their cabin bags as pillows. Third City had few simple hotels and had no room. Captain told me they had to be airborne by 7.30 am. It was almost 6 am.

I calculated that maybe one more tanker trip was needed to stop the fuel leak. I should finish by 6.30. But I had the newly created problem of filling up what was mistakenly taken out. The flight engineer told me that for flight, the current state of imbalance was out of the limits. Once the airplane was airborne, the heavier wing would drop and the airplane would cartwheel and crash. Somehow, I had to get fuel back into that wing tank. I was under tremendous strain and pressure. I was mentally and physically exhausted. There was no energy or capacity to think. The tanker came and while being filled up, the leak finally stopped. I filled the tanker completely and sent them off with huge thanks.

But the fuel imbalance remained. I could not think. I kept telling myself that I needed solutions. In an earlier call, I had asked for ideas and none came. It was pointless to make another call. I had one hour to get this airplane in the air, or we would all be here with no rooms, no fix and no help for almost two days. I didn't know what to do. I didn't know who to turn to. I sat on the top of the stairs, closed my eyes and felt the depths of despair and desperation that I had never felt before. I was on the brink of a breakdown.

I was tempted to throw in the towel. Giving up was the only option that kept coming to me. I was so tired. I knew from a previous overseas engine replacement event in the Middle East, that we were just minutes from completing a certain stage of our work when we kept hitting a brick wall. Time and time again, we tried and failed to get past a crucial stage. It was always done so easily back home. What was different now? I had realized then, that we were all tired. At that time, I called a halt, got everyone up to the airplane, put on a comedy on the movie channel and had everyone fed with sandwiches, coffee, tea and whatever refreshments they needed. After 30 minutes, we went back and got that task done at the first try.

So, I knew I was in that same place. Physically and mentally drained, I looked down at the passengers sprawled on the tarmac and I felt sad that I had let them down. I looked to the East where the sun was rising and I thought how silent and peaceful everything was and yet there was this chaos that was about to happen when I announced that there'll be no flight today. As I gazed at the dawn, a silhouette was emerging from the darkness. It was the Twin Otter. A two engine propeller airplane that was used to bring a few passengers from one island to another. In spite of the situation I faced, I smiled. A small light airplane looking up at a Giant 747 that seemed out of place…. Wait, what?!!

I sprang to my feet and scampered down the stairs. I ran to where the flight crew were sitting. "Get Up! Get up! Get the airplane ready. We are going to fly" I shouted. I turned to the local mechanic and said, "Please get me the refuel vehicle that fills up that Twin Otter. Quickly!" To everyone else I announced "Get ready for boarding!" Everyone was infected by my sense of urgency. We had less than an hour before the 7.30 am deadline was upon us. I stopped the flight engineer and said, "Please keep an eye on that fuel gauge. When we are within limits, put on the beacon light and I'll stop. I won't have time to make it exactly balanced but I will make it balanced enough to fly out safely." He grinned and nodded.

I went out over the top of the wing and when the Twin Otter refuel truck came, I got them to hand me the hose and nozzle. These light aircraft get filled up pretty much like you do with a car. The bigger airplanes were a little different, using higher pressures and secure connections. Over the top of the wings of the older 747s, are refuel caps that open directly into some of the tanks just like a car. To my knowledge, no one had ever done this before and I was dismayed that I had no camera with me. I opened the cap for the No.1 tank, put the fuel nozzle in and squeezed the trigger. Fuel came gushing out and started filling the tank. I grinned like a monkey and sat there filling her up while watching the passengers board. I looked at my watch. We were to be airborne by 7.30. Would that damn beacon light ever come on? Finally, though it seemed like forever, the beacon light came on and I wrapped up the process. The fire trucks had been hosing the underneath of the airplane since the leak had stopped and were now pulling away. It was safe to start the engines and taxi out. The paperwork was done, the doors closed, and the engines were started.

I joined them up in the flight deck as we taxied down the runway, made a 180 degree turn at the end of it, advanced the thrust levers and barreled down the runway. I looked at my watch as we lifted off. It was 7.30 am. We were all silent, maintaining strict protocol of a sterile cockpit as we climbed into the early morning. It would be three hours to Second City. At 10,000 feet, the seatbelt signs came off and I excused myself. The flight crew grinned at me and the Captain simply said, "Thank you. Go get something to eat and a bit of shut eye eh?"

I was now in desperate need of a freshen up. I was dirty, sweaty, grubby from all that running around and climbing all over the place. I did that as best as I could and made my way to my assigned seat at 1A. I sat down wearily and nodded to a passenger across the aisle at 1K. The Flight attendant came, laid the tablecloth on my meal table and gave me my breakfast. I was eager to eat for I was ravenous but before that could happen, emotions hit me without warning and I broke down and sobbed. I sobbed and sobbed, my shoulders heaving, my hands shaking as I held the napkin to my face trying my best not to make a sound. This went on for so long. The emotions, the strain, the exhaustion, the worry, the tension, frustration, hunger, thirst and fatigue and relief were all let out in those many minutes.

I don't know for how long this went on. I was suddenly conscious of a hand gently placed on my knee and another on my shoulder and I became aware of the flight attendant kneeling at my side. She didn't say a word. She didn't move and I accepted this great gesture of comfort, sympathy and human kindness. It was quite a while before my sobbing eased and my shoulders became still. I wiped my eyes and regained my composure as best as I could. I looked up at her with gratitude. She also had tears in her eyes. We smiled. By now, I was feeling a little foolish. She asked me if I was ok and I said yes. I also said I was hungry and we both laughed. She went away and I caught sight of Mr. 1K looking at me kindly. I suspect he had called her over when he saw and perhaps heard me. I nodded and tucked into my breakfast. Miss Gentle Hands came back with another serving of the main course and I hoovered that down. Then a third course and I cleaned that up as well! Eventually I could settle back and take a short nap. We would be in Second City soon. As I drifted off to sleep, I told myself, "Never, never, ever give up on anything. Always find a way. There HAS to be a way......."

12

POLITICS

Most jobs are relatively straight forward and once done repeatedly, become easy and familiar. You get it done. Hopefully you enjoy it and you learn as you pick up experience. But politics is another animal altogether. It runs along the corridors of company culture. It resides in the mindset of the individuals higher up in the food chain. It changes from individual to individual, section by section, department by department, location by location. It is set to the tune sung by the Mother of all Bosses and this modern-day Pied Piper in Corporate HQ has everybody marching to the same beat.

As you rise higher in the ranks, politics creeps in. Instead of focusing on issues, we slowly become aware of personalities. When something happens, higher ups demand to know the very minute it happens. Resolving the matter is a secondary issue but heaven help you if another boss calls your boss and your boss is clueless. He will quickly become the butt of snide remarks that permeate amongst the higher ups and you quickly find yourself in hot water because you made him look bad. While operations move at a rapid pace and situations change constantly, politics moves at the speed of thought. As fast as a text message can be sent, so do the daily fortunes rise and fall of those individuals fighting in the upper atmosphere of politics.

Fairness is not necessarily automatic, universal or guaranteed. Good work is rewarded with more work. Good work has a very short shelf life. It needs constant renewal for greater advertising recall. However, bad work comes fully packaged with preservatives. In the court of public opinion, documents and facts do not matter. When a problem occurs, people are guilty until proven guilty. In order not to incriminate yourself, sometimes no answer is better than the answer no. The attitude of quantity over quality makes people want things yesterday. And you do not want to upset the boss. Shoot the messenger first and let another clean up the mess. You do not want to be that guy who walks behind the elephant. Politicians who use you for their own advancement routinely make promises that assure the higher ups that they will try your best. So, if you don't measure up, they are well away at arm's length. Politics requires you to think of a solution but a solution that requires little or no output by your boss. Your solution cannot become his problem.

Progress makes you work hard to effect a positive change. Politics however makes you lazy and desperate. Take something that works, strip it apart, make a mess of it, put it together, use numbers to prove your case and pronounce it a change. Before the true effects can be felt, you are rewarded by a lateral or upward movement on the corporate ladder.

A thin layer of oil separates water from the atmosphere. Similarly, a thin layer of management separate you from politics.

These are your immediate managers. The ones you grew up with. They encourage you; they protect you; they guide you. They are like family. They practice tough love but shield you from the atmosphere. They want to know quickly when things go wrong so that they can find a solution. They understand that a flat tire happens when you own a car. So, they understand the difference between the man and the machine. Getting bad news early is good news. They don't want you to fall off a cliff, they tell you where the edges are. They help you realize that you have to prove on a daily basis, why you should be allowed to come back to work the next day. They guide you as you float up in life. They teach you to be fair and kind to all. The closer you get to the atmosphere, the sharper your political skills and instincts become. They teach you to write reports that go out into space and never come back. That means no fault or issues could be found. They teach you that image management is as important as actually getting the job done. Not only must it be done but it must be seen to be done. And remember - do not be the third guy. The first guy stands up and makes things happen. The second guy looks around and watches and learns as things happen. The third guy looks up and says, "What happened?".

13

HOME AGAIN

While in the midst of our overseas assignment, Angel and I bought a home. There was extensive remodeling to be done. This was all carried out via telephone and fax to our contractors with Angel going back periodically to check on the progress. Taking a home, stripping it down to its structures and building it back up with 90% transformation required detailed drawings, extensive research and complete visualization. It was a great experience putting it all together and the success or failure relied solely on the combined imaginative prowess of Angel and myself. It had to work. Nobody trains in sports to get a silver medal. Angel had completely furnished it and we moved in on Christmas Eve, 1994. It was beautiful and we lived there for 10 years. We still had our overseas assignment until March 1997 but now, Angel and Prince had a home to come to when they travelled back. Princess was born in 1996 so when we finally said goodbye to our assignment, we were a family of four.

Moving back to home base was relatively easy. Same work,

different scale. But the opportunity for short term travel was very great. I was in a pool of flyers before I left for my overseas assignment and on returning to home base, I rejoined this select group. At its peak, I would be flying an average of three times a week on short regional flights in various aircraft types to all the airports in the network that didn't have an engineer based there. I had some pretty eventful flights though. We landed twice with fire engines in attendance, we turned back after getting airborne due to faults that occurred, we rejected take offs a couple of times and we had go arounds more than once. Being in the flight deck to witness all these events made me appreciate the level of training these pilots go through and it made me proud to be a part of this airline with such professional pilots. I'd fly with them any day.

It was on one such flight about twenty years ago that sparked a change in my thinking. It was an overnight flight, 10 hours over the ocean and while in cruise, I went up to the flight deck to keep the crew company. There were just the two of them in this B747-400. Flight engineers had become redundant with the advancement of technology. We were over the ocean, on autopilot with not many airplanes in this part of the world. We were talking quietly while sipping on our juice when the captain turned to me and said, "By the way, I'm retiring next month." I looked at him with a solemn face. I didn't know what to say. I had known him for some time, we often did flights together. I felt a little sad. Most pilots love their job. It is a passion; a delightful and well-paid hobby and I imagine it would be sad to leave that all behind.

"Will you miss it?" I asked.

"Yes, of course but that's bound to happen at some point." he answered. "But what I will miss most, is a regular paycheck."

That statement was like a revelation. I kept quiet because it was so true, so sad, so full of foreboding and served as a powerful wake up call for the co-pilot and myself. How did it get to be like this? We are not trained to future proof ourselves. This subject is not taught in our education systems. Money is not taught, money management, money planning, money usage becomes the responsibility of each individual to learn the hard way. It is left to a few people who realized this gap in the Education for Life, to put together their experiences and run a course, a workshop, a webinar, write a book or take part in speaking engagements to deliver this knowledge. Their target audiences would be people like myself who, by chance, came to realize this and sought to find out more about it. When I speak of this to people now, most still think that the topic of money is premature and can be left to a more convenient time. That conversation at 35,000 feet on a moonless night changed my thinking and started a quest to find out more about what can be done sooner rather than later to avoid that sinking feeling of wondering where that next paycheck would come from.

The flying duty continued but in addition to that, short term assignments overseas came my way from time to time. It's always exciting to be asked to go someplace for a few weeks or even months to a place I had never been before. Or even to a place where I would not usually think to spend my own money to go to. Even in this small pool of flyers, politics reared its ugly head. Since I was always eager for new experiences, every time I was asked to go someplace, I would say yes. I did not stop to think of a roster system or if the other guys had their turn. That was for the bosses to manage. I kept it simple. I kept my head down, I never jockeyed into position, I always said yes to any task good and less than ideal. I said yes to both first world stations and third world, hardship, stations. But, one day, someone came up to me and peered into my eyes. "Yup," he declared, "You have blue eyes." And he abruptly tuned and went away. I was taken aback. My eyes are brown and, in our society, being a blue-eyed boy was someone who was especially favored by the higher ups. I had done nothing to attract that and the jealousy of this person was of his doing. But it taught me to be wary and watch my back.

Angel always accompanied me on my little travels and once, in 1991, we were evacuated hastily because the Gulf War had started. But all this time, I was always thinking, musing, reading about money, how it works, what do people do when they no longer have a job. Do they run a business? What about investments or the stock market? Do they own property? Do they write books or deliver lectures?

As my rocket and its assembly of platform and crawler continued on its way, I found myself asking these financial questions more and more. By now, we are about halfway along the three-mile trip to the launch pad. As I look back now, even as we continued our journey, I did not realize how eventful, significant, exciting and life changing this was all going to be.

14

ALIENS

When I was in high school, I became aware of a restlessness, an unease. A sense of being a misfit was always with me and my mind constantly drifted to thoughts of moving to another country. Nothing wrong with where I was but let's just say that instead of a nest, I preferred to stay in a field in a valley. As I grew older, my job allowed me to travel away from my nest and even stay in other nests. But I always came back to the one nest. When I met Angel, she felt the same way. Our quest to move unofficially began on our honeymoon in 1988. While in Hawaii, we studied real estate opportunities and I even looked for a job. But life got in the way. We bought a house in our nest. We were in another nest for a little more than five years. We had Prince and Princess. I got a promotion and the thought of moving to a field in a valley kept getting pushed back.

Finally, with an age limit on migration coming up, we made the decision and started the legal process. That itself was another set of hops, skips and jumps, obstacles, hula hoops and tricks we had to navigate and perform. It is no wonder then, that there are middlemen or legal migration agents to help you through the maze of legal requirements. What usually took six to eight months to complete took us two years to do successfully. In June 2003, we were granted legal ability to move to a field in a valley.

Angel stopped working when we had our children. Prince and Princess were now in grade school. I was very much entrenched in the airline, was promoted and played a great role in the operations at the New Airport. It seemed like a blink of the eye but the New Airport was by now twenty-two years old. For two years, all efforts were put into the legal process to be able to move to a field in a valley. Now that we were successful, the next step was to actually move.

The details of moving from a nest to a field in a valley can fill a book. There was no one there that we could rely on for help in getting around, learning the local rules and customs and settling in. Just as we did when we were planning the remodeling of our home in the nest, we had to do the same for this massive move. I imagined I would be working in the airport but there were two. So, we picked an area in between them. In 2003, the internet and mobile phones made the selection a little easier. There were schools there and we enrolled Prince and Princess in a suitable school. That sorted, the next thing was to find a house to rent.

The target date for the move was Dec 01, 2003. I went earlier on my own to find a temporary nest to rent. I picked a week in early November 2003 for this task. Come what may, I needed to have a contract in my hand before I left. That was the mission. First lesson in a new field in a valley - know the local festivals and happenings. There was a major event in the city that week and there was not a suitable hotel room to rent that whole week. Search as I may before I left, I could not find any. I arrived in the late evening with no pre-booked accommodation and I went to the phone book straight away.

I started at the letter A and worked my way down the alphabet. All calls were unsuccessful and by the time I reached S, I was getting pretty concerned. At the letter T, I found one person who answered sleepily and said his was a small place that had only seven rooms. Only one was left. He was located on a side street above a bar. Another person had booked that room but had not shown up. If I got there before him.... I left the phone dangling and jumped into a cab. It was well past midnight when I crawled into bed, thankful for the room and eager to begin my quest.

I began my search for a new nest in the morning. It was Monday and I was due to fly back on Friday night. I took two trains and a bus and walked into a real estate office. With a list in my hand, I walked the beat - going from house to house on that list. At lunch, I got in touch with Angel, who was looking at the same list on the computer. Even though we had mobile phones, they weren't exactly like the smart phones with all the apps that we use today. These phones in 2003 were those green screen ones with talk and text and a few simple other features. Like a bee in a field of spring flowers, I continued buzzing around in the afternoon, took a bus and two trains back to my room above a bar and slept like a rock.

Tuesday, Wednesday and Thursday went by in a flash. At lunch on Thursday, I had a fresh list from the real estate lady and while having lunch, spoke with Angel. She and I spotted a new listing almost at the same time. It was almost exactly how we spotted the listing all those years ago in 1992 for our first nest. I called the real estate lady and she agreed to come by and open the home for me to view. I loved it instantly and the location was perfect. Before I left that day, the real estate lady promised to draw up a contract in a week. I said no. I needed that contract signed the next day at midday. The real estate lady started to say something about being busy, legal needs and search my history and all that when she stopped and looked at me. She knew I had been searching the whole week and must have sensed my urgency and mission driven intensity. She nodded and told me to be back at 3 pm.

On the flight home the next evening, I held a copy of the signed rental agreement beginning Dec 01, 2003. The mission had its successful completion. I did not know then that we would end up staying there for a full five years. We were now legal aliens in a field in a valley.

15

THERE AND BACK AGAIN

We moved to the new nest. Settling in a new nest is exciting and worrying at the same time. We actually didn't know very much. First thing to do was try and remember the route to the supermarket. As time went on, we expanded our local area knowledge to include the gas stations, hairdresser, the pizza shop and the video library. It was a little lucky that at least we were driving on the same side of the road as old nest. Pretty soon, seasons changed and we were excited to experience all these things. But, in fact, all these experiences were first hand experiences by Angel and the children. I was still a butterfly. At the time we moved to new nest in a field in a valley, the valley was in a drought. I could not find a job there, so I never actually left my original job back in old nest.

We did the next best thing. Angel ran the household while I went back to work. During school holidays, I would fly over to new nest and then back to old nest when holidays were over. This was difficult. It was heartbreaking. I had ten weeks to mend my heart, build up hope and excitement only to have my heart broken every time I had to leave them. I did try using Skype but after two Skype calls, I stopped using Skype and never touched it again for 15 years. It was doubly heartbreaking to be able to see them and not hug them. So, for the next six years, I was pretty much a butterfly flying in and out every so often. I got to know the menus on the flights, the timings by heart and since I was flying on a standby basis, I knew the seasons where getting a seat would be best. I would work the whole day, jump on a flight after my duty ended and then fly back at the end of the school holidays to arrive a couple of hours before my duty started.

The financials for such a move was not something I had thought out well enough. I had a household running in the new nest. There was rent, utility bills, household expenses and all of life's usual needs. The cost of living was higher in new nest. I was still earning money in old nest and the exchange rate did not help me at all. When I was looking for a bank in the new nest, I researched the financial magazines and found out which bank had the award for the best internet portal. I found out that the internet and usage of IT in new nest was not what I was used to in old nest. I chose that bank and have not regretted it one bit. I needed such an efficient banking portal because I had to be moving money across to new nest regularly and paying bills from where I was in old nest. Angel could not help me in this as we had no internet in the new house in new nest. The iPhone and all those apps didn't make their appearances until 2007.

Back in old nest, I still had a mortgage, I still had the usual house bills in old nest, albeit a little less now. But it was silly to be having two bills to pay for. But we planned to ship all our furniture by sea to new nest instead of buying fresh items that would have cost more. So right when I was facing all this set up and moving costs, I received a letter from the IRS. When you get a letter from the IRS out of the blue, it is never a lottery or a windfall. I read their letter with dismay. Back in the year 2000 when I did my taxes, they replied that I owed them $0 for that year. I was happy and assumed it was certain benefits and claims that I had put in and that as a family of four we were entitled to.

Big mistake. Never ever assume. If it looks and smells good, it's probably not good. And true enough, it didn't taste good. Now here in January 2004, they sent me a whoopsie daisy letter telling me that their systems were in error and that I owed them a full year in back taxes and they wanted it in one hit. Having used up our money for the move, the rent and all those things, I was now preparing money for the shipment of the furniture when this letter came. Here now come the lessons in negotiations, money management, resource allocation, scheduling timely disbursements and resolving funding challenges. In plain simple English, I begged the IRS for a repayment plan. I even offered to pay interest (I was desperate) and made sure not to tell them it was their mistake to begin with. I cashed in an old insurance plan that I had forgotten about which went straight into paying for the packing and shipment of our furniture to new nest. Angel agreed to defer buying a car in new nest for six months until we got through this patch. They agreed to take the buses and trains. I reduced all scheduled payments to minimum to try and improve my cashflow . I actually lost a little weight in going easy on meals.

After all the moving was completed, I sold the car that we had and took buses and trains myself. In the tax system of old nest, we paid our taxes for the previous year on a monthly basis in the following year. That usually took up 25% of my net income. Now with the back taxes of the year that was missed, a princely 50% of my net income went straight out to taxes. Taking out rent for new nest and mortgage on old nest, and all other recurring expenses, I had no more than $5 in my wallet at any one time that entire year.

So, you learn. You move on carefully. You examine every expense. You try to predict upcoming expenses and search for another way to bring in the extra income. One way that I knew of but could not do straight away, was to rent out our home in old nest. Before I could do that, I needed to do a little cosmetic work to spruce it up and make it look pretty for prospective tenants. That needed money. In saving for the money to do this, I was losing potential revenue in rental. I was between a rock and a hard place. But as soon as I could, I put the house up for rental. In the meantime, I rented a room near work and yes that was another expense I had to bear for a little while. But, soon enough, I had a family interested in old house and they moved in. It was such a relief to have a tenant as they paid the equivalent of the 50% that I had been paying the IRS. Immediately, my cash flow bounced up and with that, things started to look up. My stress levels went down as fast as my weight went back up.

I now had the first taste of what a cosmetic renovation could bring me. I had the first-hand experience of being a landlord with positive cashflow. I had the experience once again of being in a rut and being forced to find multiple elusive solutions. The questions on finance that I had started to ask myself a few years ago had taken a back seat to the process to move to a new nest in a field in the valley. Now that things were beginning to settle down, these questions flared up again and I found myself reading books and magazines on the subject at the best time available to me. In flight.

16

THE LONE RANGER IN OLD NEST

I used the months and years in old nest to work hard. My regular work was getting mentally challenging. I was moving towards management rather than work on airplanes individually. I had to manage people, flights, reports and had all the obstacles of running a complex, ever changing environment. No two days were alike although some of the problems were the same, just either bad or worse. The style of running an airline was moving to one of management by numbers. Clever people who never saw the sun were telling us how things should be done and that usually doesn't go down well. Operational meetings in the morning were reduced to finger pointing and assigning blame. Once again, we had to learn a new language. Just as I had learnt the language of money way back in 1984, we now had to learn the language of statistics. You cannot manage or argue a case if you do not know or have the numbers.

That became the tone of the early 2000s. All departments were reduced to producing data and reports and figures for someone to read while the people right there in the thick of it, were facing logistical and practical problems that the figures did not show. More and more clever people were recruited or promoted to manage this huge amount of data and statistics . Fewer and fewer people were left to do the actual physical work. This gap between reality and theory was frustrating for us and widened as time went on. The most maddening event for me was when a clever chap took a system that was working so well, ripped it apart, made it more complex, created more middle management jobs and all for a 7% increase in manpower usage. Work efficiency fell 25% but no one admitted to that. My work partner and I discussed this at length when we came across that topic of retirement and, for me, the creation of the rocket and stage theory of our lives.

My place of solitude and peace was both my little rented room and my seat at the pointy end of the airplane when I did my flying duties. Since all flying duties were done on our days off, I earned more for this. This helped in the cashflow and the building up of funds. Since I was alone in old nest, what else could I do but work? I read as much as I could. I went from one author to the next. Finance, self-help, property, the stock market, investments of one nature or another. It was quite a world I had opened up for myself. Since I was busy exchanging time for money, I had not the presence of mind to make my money work for me. Not yet anyway. Simple reason, I did not have much money. I also enjoyed the first run movies on board so that too kept me both entertained and distracted.

The other thing I did have time for was exercise. I swam 40 laps of an Olympic swimming pool twice a week. I would take my road bike out at night when it was cooler with less traffic and cleaner air and ride sometimes till dawn. Being in a 24/7 industry, I worked days and nights and the best riding would be at the end of a day shift and swim before a night shift. No exercise on flying days. It was on one such occasion in the evening of Feb 7, 2008 when I took my bike out for a night ride.

I usually cycled on bike paths well away from road traffic. I didn't trust the drivers to do the right thing. All my riding was kept to established paths just for riding. It was almost midnight on this day when I reached a straight stretch of road. I could see ahead of me about 300 yards and there was another cyclist coming towards me. It was just the two of us and it was normal to be riding in opposite directions in this two-way bike path. As our distance apart closed in, I noticed he was a little unsteady and was not cycling in a straight line. I slowed but just a little and I kept an eye on him. He looked to be steadying up a little and I relaxed a bit. So, it was with shock and horror when just as we were about to safely pass each other, he swerved into my path and fell.

17

CRASH AND RECOVERY

Without thinking, I hit both brakes of my bike. The front wheel locked and I flew over my bike, catching my shin and my bike shorts on my own handlebars and flew straight ahead and landed very heavily on my left shoulder and then scraped my left elbow, hip and thigh. I felt something rip in my shoulder and I knew it was not good. I lay there for a few seconds and looked around. The unsteady cyclist was nowhere to be seen. He had vanished. I lay back to take stock of what had happened and then slowly used my right hand and felt all around my body to see if I was bleeding anywhere. When all seemed in order, I tried to sit up. I couldn't. A bus came by and stopped 20 feet from me and a couple of people stepped out. They walked my way and I called out for help. To my surprise and disgust, they looked away and actually stepped out onto the road, avoided me and stepped back in and went on their way. I muttered my thoughts and wished them a week of constant diarrhea.

Again, I tried to sit up. Nothing happened. My left arm was useless. I dragged myself along the ground to the safety railings nearby and used my right hand to pull myself up into a sitting position. My bike lay in a heap, my left leg was bleeding, my bike shorts was torn and my left arm was just dead weight and completely immobile. I used my right hand to lift my left hand across my stomach and used my left thumb to hook on to my riding belt. I slowly pulled myself up to stand and when all stopped spinning, walked slowly to pick up my bike and locked it to the rails. I needed to get to the hospital and hoped for a passing taxi. One came and didn't stop. Then another and another. When they saw that I was in bike clothes and maybe looking a little messed up, they just drove on. I was getting quite fed up and when the next taxi came by, I stepped out on the road and did my best to halt him. He did. I held up my mobile phone as if to record his license plate and he watched me warily as I approached.

Since it was past midnight, there were no other cars. Otherwise, I would not have done this at all. We drove to the hospital in silence. Most people would have asked what happened or how I was, but taxi man said nothing. Well that was fine, I guess. At least I had a ride. I walked into the Emergency room and they took my details politely. As I sat there, people were being brought in on gurneys bleeding all over, in great pain and obviously in far worse condition than I was. Looking at all that, I was grateful I could at least walk in on my own bleeding leg. Eventually I was seen and an x-ray showed all ligaments in my shoulder were torn. There was nothing connecting the bones of my upper arm to the rest of the skeletal system except skin and muscle. My left arm was put in a sling, my wounds were dressed and I was sent home with a date for surgery and two months off work.

18

THE UNIVERSE WORKS FUNNY

Within a week, surgery was done and I stayed home briefly to rest. I found this difficult as I could not do the usual things properly. Eating was an amusing exercise as I learnt to open soda cans with one hand, balance food trays and remembered to only take either a fork or a spoon. It was useless having both. I learnt to dress myself with one hand learning right away to choose clothes with no buttons as you couldn't button anything without both thumbs. So, track pants and tee shirts were the dress code and slip on shoes with no laces as well. It's amazing how we take the use of both hands and arms for granted. It was also quite touching as the usual people I met when I went to the food places to eat, now became my helpers as they poured drinks for me, brought my food tray to me and altogether treated me like their invalid son. I didn't cook at home as rented room's owner ate special food and I didn't want to offend by risking mixing mine up with his.

When the stitches were out, I decided to fly home to our nest in the field. Angel had remained there with the children while I had my operation and she was anxious to see me. I too needed their company. So, I found myself airborne in no time. My boss objected to this saying medical leave was for me to rest and not go on what he called "a vacation." I asked him where else should I be resting? "At home!" He declared. I smiled and asked him where he thought my home was. I just love it when people are introduced to a new perspective and their world opens up a little. "Mmmm. Have a safe flight," he said, "and keep your phone on!"

While I was away, I got a text message from Middle Manager 1. He knew I was away and wanted to see me as soon as I got back to work. In the meantime, Middle Manager 2 was also looking for me, knew where I was and decided not to disturb and waited for me to return as well. So, when I returned to work, I went and met with Middle Manager 1.

"We have just won a contract" he exclaimed excitedly. "It's to help prepare for and manage a fleet of new airplanes that Valley Airlines had bought." He knew I had moved my family to a field in a valley and that meant that I had the right to work in that valley. "Would you like to manage this project?" He asked. "You will manage it from here but will have to commute to Valley Airlines Headquarters as well as several other fields in the valley where these airplanes will fly to. Oh, and by the way, we've also bought a local company in the valley and you will bring them up to speed so that they can manage these new airplanes for Valley Airlines as well."

It took me two seconds to say yes. That changed my world forever. There was so much to think and to plan and prepare for. I walked out of Middle Manager 1's office with my head full of thoughts, plans and checklists. And I bumped into Middle Manager 2. "Ah ha! You're back! Glad I caught you. I want you to be a part of a team here to look after...." And I stopped him and said, "I'm sorry. I have just agreed to a project with Middle Manager 1." I explained what had just transpired and he had a few choice words for Middle Manager 1 stealing me away. But he understood what it meant for me and he wished me luck. It turned out a few years later, Middle Manager 2 would himself be assigned to the Valley to manage our business there and we had the opportunity to work together after all. As usual, given a bit of time, good things will happen.

19

LASTING TIES

With just under a mile to go to the launch pad, it's appropriate to write about some of the people who have been following my rocket. Mom and Dad had always supported me unconditionally. While my sister was grappling with law school, she and I often studied together in the libraries. That helped me focus a lot. My parents realized that I was forging a path that was unconventional, unknown, unsafe and untested. Everyone else followed a set path that seemed to be the norm and to veer away was unheard of. Yet, they supported and encouraged me every step of the way. I didn't learn until much, much later, that my Dad had to endure a lot of teasing and sometimes insults from his colleagues about my chosen path. He kept that all to himself and didn't tell me until I was well and truly successful. It was a sickening cultural or societal habit of comparing the progress of the children of each other and some whose children did not measure up were derided and made fun of. I was grateful that he carried this burden silently as I had my own demons to manage.

I have said before, morale is very fragile and I certainly would not have welcomed that information at all. Mom was always there to confide in when I had issues that I was dealing with. She listened very well. They could not always come up with solutions for these were unique problems, but they prayed very, very hard for me and always encouraged me.

Apart from my parents and my only sister, there are a couple of people whom I've known since grade and high school. The three of us have been through a lot together and still remain together to this day. Time and space had separated us but thanks to the internet and messaging apps on our phones, we have a mini group of three and can be reached across time zones as we each traveled around the world.

I've known Catter-Stroff since the first grade. His Mom was a teacher in the first grade and taught me that hell existed on earth as well. Today, she is retired and is still a sweet lady. Catter-Stroff got his nickname when he was speaking in an animated way and mispronounced the word "catastrophe." Although we were not always in the same class, we grew up together and eventually made it to the same high school. Separated by choice of subjects, we ended up in the same interest group and continued our adventures together.

That's when we met Cheeky Grin. Cheeky Grin and I were in the same class all through high school. He was in the same interest group as Catter-Stroff and I and the three of us became firm friends. We went to each other's homes and got to know each other's families. This bond didn't change when we left high school. I joined the airline and they went on to college. We'd camped together, swam, watched movies, talked about girls like the experts we weren't and in between all our busy early lives, stayed in touch throughout. Catter-Stroff went to college in Hawaii and Washington State and Cheeky Grin went to Newcastle, England and I visited them with my handy airline tickets.

Nothing exciting happened when I visited Catter-Stroff because he has always been a sensible, levelheaded, dead-pan intellectual with the makings of a Monk. But, while in England with Cheeky Grin, a simple walk in the snow almost went horribly wrong. Cheeky Grin had grown older, became very smart but had never grown up. Always mischievous, always jumping then looking, he was impetuous, fun loving, totally honest, said what he thought and the life of every party.

One Sunday morning, on the way home from the grocery store, a snowball hit us in the back. A few burly lads had walked past us earlier and one of them decided to aim a snowball at us and he found his mark. Cheeky Grin immediately turned around and before I could tell him to ignore it, he hurled a couple of choice words at them. Well, you might as well smack a beehive while wearing speedos. They were immediately incensed. They came striding back, found empty bottles lying on the sidewalk, picked them up, smashed the bottoms out and came right at us with the sharp ends of the bottles pointing straight at us.

We stopped dead in our tracks and faced them. With grocery bags in our hands, we had no hope of defending ourselves, running or doing anything except talk our way out of this. What were we to do? Smack them with marshmallows? Once again, the basic requirement for a successful negotiation is to approach from a position of strength and in that we were not. Two skinny lads with apples, bread and milk were no match for three burly dudes with broken bottles. You size up your situation, assess your options and immediately take bold, decisive action. So, we begged, apologized, acknowledged their superiority and our unworthiness and swore never to offend them again. We accepted their verbal abuse with humility, we tolerated their insults and we just wished them away. After having pumped up their pride, fluffed up their egos, restored their masculinity, they ditched the bottles, turned and left. Cheeky Grin and I didn't say a word and waited until they were out of sight before we turned and made our way back home. He wished he had kept his mouth shut and I wished those fellas a week of stomach flu. They probably grew up to be bullies intimidating patrons at a seedy nightclub. But we came away much wiser, unscathed and with our beauty and pimples intact. Pick your battles, negotiate from strength and drop those bloody groceries and run at the first sign of trouble. My Krav Maga instructor would have been ashamed.

In April 1984, Cheeky Grin asked if I could take pictures for a family event. His parents were celebrating their 25th wedding anniversary the following month and he needed a photographer. I agreed immediately. They have always been a second family to me.

So it was that I found myself in their family home that I have come to know so well, with my camera, rolls of film, spare batteries, tripod and my coveted possession - a zoom lens. I had spent a whole months' salary on that lens which I used primarily for photographing wildlife and airplanes. I positioned myself at the top of their elliptical, elevated driveway so that I could record the arrival of all the guests as they appeared from the street down below. As I sat, pressed back into the hedge, I recorded the arrivals and the happy greetings of all the family members as they arrived. I had a sweeping view of the driveway, the gardens, the patio and as it was a perfect evening with fine weather, people mingled about and seemed reluctant to be in the house. I tried to blend in and remain as unnoticed as possible and hoped the guests would not see or notice or remember that I was there and it was my duty to be a fly on the wall.

I had most of the guests in view when I realized another family had arrived. One by one they emerged from below the horizon of the driveway: the parents, the two sons, the two elder daughters and lastly, the youngest daughter. Eagerly looking around at the familiar faces of family members already there, with a beautiful smile, perfectly coiffed hair swept back, matching earrings and elegant necklace, she was an Angel. Through the lens, I followed her every step, listened to every word, took in that lovely smile and pretty much decided that I had taken enough pictures of everyone else, focused on studying this Angel. I soon learnt that she was Cheeky Grin's first cousin. His Mom and her Dad were siblings. When I left that evening, I couldn't stop thinking about her.

Six weeks later, Angel and I had our first date. I borrowed my Dad's car and waited near her home 30 minutes early. I had planned to arrive at the gate precisely at 7 pm, whisk her away and spend the evening at dinner. So, with the precision of a Swiss watch, I arrived outside the gate. But her sister popped her head out and asked me to come in. I was horrified! I was a shy, introverted skinny guy and I was not prepared to meet more than one new person at a time. Sure enough, the whole family were there and this felt like I was ambushed into an interview. I faced seven family members, a son-in-law and a baby. I can't remember what I said or what was asked but I must have gotten their initial approval for I was then offered a coke - with ice!

Pretty soon I was let off the hook and Angel and I got back in my Dad's car and we set off. First lesson - do your research. Angel asked where we were going for dinner and I proudly announced a restaurant that I thought was appropriate (given my humble wages). Angel laughed heartily and said that restaurant was at the bottom of her office building. Of all the places in the city I could have chosen, I was now bringing her back to her work place, on a weekend, on our first date. Angel was gracious. She didn't mind. It was a good enough place and I obviously didn't know. We ended up having a good meal and chatted happily throughout. As we were about to leave, Angel went to the restroom and as she walked away, I looked at her and said to myself, "Someday, she could be my wife".

I proposed to Angel on Valentine's day two years later and we were engaged on her 21st birthday a couple of months after. A further two years passed before we were married. Cheeky Grin became my best man and second sister was Angel's bridesmaid. Later on, both of them became godparents to Prince and then, second brother and eldest sister became godparents to Princess.

20

LIFE IN THE VALLEY

With this new contract in place, I quickly realized that the timeline given was grossly inadequate. Given the amount of preparation needed, the fast approaching delivery of the airplanes, the need for budgeting and lead time for purchasing equipment, training the staff and obtaining regulatory approvals, this project should have started six months earlier. So, the learning curve was not just steep, it was almost vertical. I worked from my office in new airport, dealing with the clients in the valley, with our heads of departments in the different fields in the valley and with many other sections within the airline and the regulatory authorities in the valley. It was such a mammoth task coordinating all of these, running parallel timelines, gant charts, budgets, equipment purchasing, dozens of emails daily, conference calls. Given the time differences between places, fourteen-hour days became normal.

It became necessary for me to travel to meet with our clients and department heads in the Valley. Working all day, jumping on a plane at night, heading for meetings on arrival, then flying to the next field for another meeting. It was hectic, a blur of places, faces and events. Conversation was recorded in a series of notes, minutes were transcribed in airport waiting rooms, reports were sent before bed and the process repeated all over again before flying back at night to new airport, having a shower and a shave before heading straight to work again. Thank goodness for flat beds on airplanes.

Only once in a while did I manage to divert my trips to visit Angel and the children and this was just for the weekend before heading back. In a sense, I saw them a little more frequently than before albeit for a lesser duration. Still I welcomed any chance to see them.

Four months into the project, my repaired left shoulder snapped again and this time, the original ligaments that were precariously sewn back could not be reused. My left arm returned to the sling while a donor ligament was sourced. I learned to type with one hand very well and the speed dial function and voice commands on my phone were put to good use. A second operation was conducted with the help of a donor ligament and metal washers and this time, it became a permanent solution. I did, however, have to be ginger and careful and although I still travelled, I had to take things a little slowly. Only just. The clients were astounded when I turned up for meetings with my arm in a sling and appreciated the effort. This endeared me to them, and we soon became friends at a personal level, and this continues to this day.

Each day, there are a series of challenges. Sometimes you fall back two steps. You get up, you keep going. I reported directly to the Son of all Bosses. He was strict, demanding and exact. From him, I learned very quickly that bad news early was good news. He expected things to fumble every now and then. What he wanted to have, was the time to find a solution. Time gave him avenues and options. Time gave him a way to think up responses and back up plans. If something went wrong and you tried within your means to get it fixed and found out you couldn't and then went to him when it was too late, you might as well have released the Kraken.

I had seen Son of all Bosses in great fury when an underling made that mistake. He was swiftly chewed up and spat out. Chewy wasn't bright and didn't get the memo. He would return the next day with another bungle and there'll be these vomit noises as Son of all Bosses spat him out again. Many people feared Son of all Bosses and they reacted that way - conceal and not reveal for fear of being chewed and spat out. What they didn't understand was that Son of all Bosses was teaching us very valuable lessons. Know your limits. Be truthful. Have courage to speak out. Do your homework. Understand that precise cut off time when you have run out of your depth and still give others the chance to help. These are important life and business lessons.

Son of all Bosses was the Boss of well, Boss and Smaller Boss. So it was that Son of all Bosses had an idea to transform our core operations center. It was to be called IMOC. (Aye-mock). It was the acronym for an Integrated something or other Centre. Some mid-level muggle who had been to a clever school had drawn up the plans without consulting the users of the Centre and the end result was silly, inefficient, chaotic and embarrassing. Weeks after it was in operation, Son of all Bosses called us into a meeting to get our feedback.

Having had the reputation of chewing and then spitting people out, no one really gave any real feedback and some even dared suggest it was a success. As usual, I just kept quiet and looked down. I caught Smaller Boss's eye and he seemed to implore that I hold my tongue. I was happy to oblige until once again, I was called on directly, this time by Son of all Bosses, to speak my mind.

I started to explain exactly what the issues were. From location to efficiency to communications to noise level and the list went on. Smaller Boss had his hands in is head and the muggle who designed it was collecting neckties to hang himself. Son of all Bosses looked at me intently without saying a word. I offered alternatives, suggested solutions and even presented several role models in the industry and other high-risk operating centers to learn from and model upon. I finished soon enough and he asked me for one final thought. Here's when I should have probably shut up, but I didn't. I told him the IMOC that he had envisioned, had become an eye sore and a mockery.

Smaller Boss groaned and shook his head. Others gasped. Clever muggle had clutched his chest and started to make choking noises. Son of all Bosses did nothing but continued to look at me. Soon a wry smile came over his lips and he looked at Smaller Boss and simply said, "I like that." Son of all Bosses looked back at me and said, "Colin, I want you to always speak your mind, no matter what. I am counting on you to give me the truth".

Sadly, there are very few people who think this way. Very often, ego steps in and people get offended and you walk a tight rope trying to balance truth with politics. I haven't learned yet and I still have the habit of saying it like it is. In subsequent dealings with various groups of people, I have sought out only those who speak the truth and who are willing to listen to the truth. No cover ups, sweet language or face-saving nonsense. And always without fail, address the problem or the behavior and never the individual.

21

DESPERATE TIMES

One of the problems I recognized early on was the lack of suitably qualified people to manage those airplanes in the Valley when they did arrive. That would be unthinkable, having the airplanes turn up and be immediately grounded with no one to certify them. There was no shortage of qualified people here in new airport but there were no local people in the Valley who could do that as no one else had yet brought this type of airplane into the Valley.

While we had already begun training the locals, they would be ready only after the airplane had arrived. So, a plan was made to select and train seven people, including myself, to take our qualifications in new airport and go through the legal process of converting our licenses into licenses issued by the authorities from the Valley. There were a few subjects we had to learn and be tested on and arrangements were made for that to happen. There were also other legalities to be performed and a plan was drawn to have all these formalities done in a week.

Remember my mission way back to find a home to rent within a week? Well this took on the mission status in the exact same way. We had five days to complete the courses and take the exams and have our new airport papers ratified and legally accepted in the Valley, submit all of them before we left at the end of the week. The aim was for a successful completion - the dual Mission objectives.

We arrived in one of the fields in the valley on Sunday night. All seven of us began our quest the next morning. We ended the day quite late each day. By Friday afternoon, we had completed every task except one. This final task was to have our papers ratified by the local authorities. In my own field in the valley, there were several ways to have this done. I did not realize that in THIS field in the valley, there were only two ways to have this done and one of them finished for the day at 2 pm. It was now 4 pm.

I was horrified. I did not realize that my many options were now reduced to one. And this one was a long shot. I was now seeking, a Part-time Justice of the Peace who would be willing to assist us on a Friday evening. The other six were dismayed and assumed all was lost. We had accomplished all our tasks and were due to fly back to new airport the next morning. I asked all to return to their rooms, keep a listening watch while I worked this out.

As before, letting the mission fail was not acceptable. I sat with my laptop open in my hotel room and searched the internet for a part-time Justice of the Peace in the region we were in. There were 18. All with addresses and telephone numbers. I started ringing. Out of town. Wrong number. Disconnected. No longer doing this. Unable. Too late. Who are you again and do you know what time it is? I went down the list and quickly reached number 17. A lady answered. I quickly begged for help. I explained our plight and told her what I had done to reach the sixteen people before her and that I had only one more number on my list and if she failed me so might the last one and then I would be a complete and utter failure....She said ok. I said "what??" Stupidly and scarcely believing my luck, I heard her as she said it again, "OK." She said to come over, gave me the address and I thanked her profusely. I group messaged the others to meet me in the lobby STAT. (I don't know what that means. All those ER people in the movies say that a lot. I guess it means to hurry.)

And hurry we did. We got there in 20 minutes and this kind middle aged lady came down from her apartment in a dressing gown with her hair in curlers. She brought a pen, an ink pad and a stamp. She was amused to see seven desperate faces. After greeting us, Snow White began to take page by page, checking the originals and stamping and signing the copies. One by one for each of us. All of us waited in the lobby and gave Snow White a little space and we spoke in low tones or checked our phones as you do. It was almost midnight when she let out a sigh and stood up. By then, we were all weak with hunger, tired from the long day and badly needing to pee. Snow White handed our precious documents back to us, accepted our heartfelt thanks and bade us a cheery farewell. By law, she was not allowed to accept anything from us except our thanks. So we parted.

The guys were ecstatic. More than one of them thought the game was over and that we could not complete the mission. I hoped that this lesson gave them the encouragement to keep thinking, keep fighting and never give up anything that was worth fighting for. The next morning, we handed in our papers to the authorities. I had been keeping Son of all Bosses in the loop in my daily messages with him. So just before we boarded the flight, I sent one final message: "Done."

22

LAUNCH PAD

With just a hundred yards to go, Launch Pad loomed above us. The hurdles we had encountered in getting ready were a real challenge each and every time. Nothing good or worth its salt was ever going to be easy and this was no different. By now, most of the processes were in place. Most of the drills and dress rehearsals had been done. The people were in place. The airplanes were getting ready to be delivered and flown out. All the planning, visualization, policies and procedures were drawn out. I myself was making my own preparations to leave new airport and move to new nest in a field in the valley. It was agreed that when the airplanes arrived, it was no longer practical for me to remain in new airport and run the operations from there. And since I had my own home and family in the Valley, it made sense for me to transfer the flag and set up shop in country.

So it was that after six years of separation and commuting to be with my family, I finally arrived home for good. The children had grown. They were both in high school. Angel had started working again as soon as Princess had left the sixth grade. I had a lot of catching up to do. I had tried to come home when a significant event in school was taking place but did miss some. I was able to be there for every birthday and every Christmas. It was a precious time. I will never know if the separation had had any permanent adverse effects in my relationship with my family, but I certainly would not wish separation on anybody. But, thankfully, that period was over, and it was time to rebuild and move ahead.

I was not living in the valley on vacation. The project was just taking off and the airplanes had arrived. The legalities were being performed and everyone was getting ready for first flight. This meant that I was again shuttling between different fields in the valley. For the purposes of clarity and understanding, let's call them Field A, Field B and Field C. Valley Airlines HQ was in Field A. The launch city was from Field B. The airplanes were destined to fly only between Field B and way over the ocean to a different field in a Mountain. This field in the Mountain we shall call Field L. Field L was started by Middle Manager 1 himself way back when he first spoke to me. He landed in Field L with a suitcase and a cell phone. By now, he had set up a whole base of operations in this field in a mountain and it was bigger than Fields A, B and C combined. Middle Manager 1 did very well indeed.

The plan was for Valley Airlines to launch from Field B and fly to Field L. After a few months, as more airplanes arrived, they would start from Field A and fly to Field L. No plans to operate from Field C. My instructions were to prepare for operations from Fields B and A. So, I was to budget for equipment for fields B and A only. The equipment to gear up these two fields had a lead time of six months. This meant that it would take six months from ordering and paying before the equipment would be delivered. I wondered how long a lead time I would be given to gear up for Field C should they change their minds.

Valley Airlines had been in operation for three months and they were an instant success. They provided the travelling public with an alternative to Incumbent Airlines that had been operating and enjoying the monopoly for so long. So successful was Valley Airlines that they decided to start flying from Field C. I had five weeks notice.

It was good timing that we had our quarterly business meeting in Field A at about the time Valley Airlines decided to start flying from Field C. Son of all Bosses was there together with Middle Manager 1, myself and a few others. Valley Airlines Engineering Manager made this announcement and all at the table let out a collective gasp including his own people. Valley Airlines asked one question, "Will we be ready?" Son of all Bosses knew exactly the timelines and the lead time it would take to procure the equipment and he looked at me with a little pain in his eyes. I nodded, looked back at Valley Manager and said simply, "Yes".

After the meeting was over, the usual drinks and dinner followed. When the hosts had departed and we had returned to our hotel, we held a short meeting. Naturally, Son of all Bosses wanted to know why I said yes given that we had only five weeks to prepare and the authorities would have to come to audit Field C in three weeks. Middle Manager 1 was sympathetic for he had his own issues, but he too was curious. I looked around the table and for the first time in my relationship with Son of all Bosses, I decided to keep him and everyone else out of the loop.

There is a term called Plausible Deniability, used in both business and politics. Simply put, this usually meant that an underling had done something slightly or greatly illegal but didn't tell the boss about it. So, if questioned, the boss could honestly testify that he had no prior knowledge of this activity. In my time spent in this contract and possibly my time spent on Earth, I have learnt to be as prepared as possible for any eventuality. Airlines run at the speed of thought and since they were run by Marketing and Finance, little or no regard is given to the logistical requirements of Engineering. Especially Engineering that had been outsourced as we had. "Get it done" would be their expectation. No thought, knowledge or sympathy was given to our "difficult lead times."

I had to prepare a white paper and do a budget and costing exercise to explain why I needed $X million dollars to buy equipment for Field B and Field A. I had presented this paper to the Board several months before in the lead up to getting Field B and Field A up and running. With all the equipment in place, they passed the audit and were now operational. Suddenly Valley Airlines wanted to operate from Field C. So, way back then, I actually prepared a budget to buy 1.5 times the equipment I needed in each of the Fields B and A. If I needed two such items in Field B, I would budget to buy three. I did the same for Field A. I actually ended up with a full complement of Field C's equipment housed separately in both Fields B and A.

Now the time had come for me to collect. I sent out a list of equipment to both managers of Fields B and A and asked them to send these items to Field C. Within a week, Field C had its full complement of equipment and we waited patiently for the Audit. Soon enough, I messaged Son of all Bosses. "Audit passed. Field C ready." I was pleased and Son of all Bosses was relieved. The client was delighted.

23

THE TWO MINUTE COUNTDOWN BEGINS

My rocket was now sitting securely on the launch pad. It was being fueled and made ready for launch. The tests continued. The failures were being addressed and daily checks, practices, reports, and meetings took up all the time. Impatient managers demanded more and more. Clients expected hoop jumping to be a norm and thanks to my Blackberry, I was on call 24/7. Staff were helping as much as they could, but they had their limits. After three years managing the contract with Valley Airlines, I handed it over to another person in Field A.

I started to manage Field C and overlooked matters in Field B and yet another place, Field D. At about this time, we had another contract, this time with Animal Airlines. Animal Airlines was a low-cost outfit that insisted on paying 50 cents but demanded ten dollars worth of quality. They were cheats, liars, paid late and were the most dishonest and unreasonable people in business I had ever met. It was quite a culture shock as I did not expect this behavior from within a first world country.

Animal Airlines and another, Arrogant Airlines, took up almost all my time. The many other airlines that we also managed were a nice bunch but my whole corporate world and my private and family time were all consumed by both Animal and Arrogant Airlines.

It felt for so long, that we always took two steps forward and fell back three. This went on for so many years, it was akin to running underwater. If you have ever had the chance to try this, it is basically putting in a lot of effort and getting nowhere. To say that we as a company were running around in circles is an understatement. The trio of troubles was made complete when our parent company in New Airport expected us to run our business with the same conditions and business model as in New Airport. Things were different in the Valley. The laws, cost of living, business environment and competition were totally different from New Airport. Pricing points, Labour Union activity and the cost of compliance were far greater than Mother of all Bosses and the rest at New Airport ever understood. So besides running underwater, we now had to do it handcuffed. The demands of Animal and Arrogant Airlines were incessant. In July 2013, I developed chest pains.

I mentioned this to a dear friend of mine in the office and he asked why I was still at the airport and not at the doctor's. He threatened to press the off button on my laptop if I didn't get out and go see the doctor. I did that and the doctor sent me straight to the Emergency Room of the nearest hospital. I spent the whole day undergoing tests and by late evening, I was allowed to go home but had to return several times the following few days to do further tests. After almost two weeks, I was given a clean bill of health and I heaved a huge sigh of relief. I did ask the cardiologist what could have caused those chest pains for I certainly did not imagine them. He asked what my daily routine was and I told him. He said simply, "Stress."

I went home and told Angel what the cardiologist had said. We were both quiet. I knew what I needed to do and she knew it too, but she wanted for me to say it. And I did. "I need to step away from all this otherwise the next time I have chest pains, it will be for real."

But it was not my choice. A new General Manager had taken over and his task was to turn the company around and stem the losses. He asked me to cut staffing levels by 40%. I felt that it would put staff and airplanes in danger. It was too much, too soon. The contract with Animal Airlines would be over in less than six months and we could re-look those numbers again then. He refused. Having brought in his own HR manager into the company only days before, he removed me from my post and installed a friend of his in my place. After 35 years painstakingly climbing the corporate ladder, I was made an engineer once again.

24

THE FINAL TEN.

TEN......

I had so much time off due to me, I went off work for four months. Angel, Prince, Princess and I went on a seven-week vacation including a week at sea on a cruise. We also made a special visit to Arlington National Cemetery in Virginia. My goal was to visit the grave of President John F. Kennedy with the eternal flame that I had read so much about. This was the man whose assassination was one of my very first memories all those many, many years ago. It was a somber visit and I had forgotten that it was this man who started my interest in rockets, airplanes and led me to a career that would span almost 40 years.

NINE......

It was as if a huge weight had been lifted off from my shoulders. For the first time in six years, I didn't have to check my email every time the Blackberry buzzed. I stopped having phone calls throughout the day and night. I stopped having people texting me at 4 am saying they couldn't come to work at 6 am. I stopped working seven days a week. I swore that the next time I went into business, I would do it myself and would outsource everything and have zero staff. I returned from the four months off and went back to work as an aircraft engineer. All I had to remember was when I needed to come back to work the next day. It was bliss. I had forgotten how it was with airplanes. They were still the sweetest things and we still looked after them carefully. The contract with Animal Airlines was over and that was a huge relief. I never wanted to have anything to do with them ever again. Arrogant Airlines was still Arrogant, but they were now someone else's problem.

EIGHT......

I no longer had to travel frequently to Field B and Field D. I remained in Field C and that was most agreeable for I was with my family 100% of the time. We went on another family vacation in 2014 and this was as happy and as memorable as the one before including another week at sea. Part of this trip was a visit to Dallas, Texas. I wanted to see the place in Dealey Plaza, the route of the Presidential motorcade and visit the sixth floor of the then Texas School Book Depository. All these places are connected with the death of President John F. Kennedy on November 22, 1963. Once again, I took it all in and spent time reading all the various accounts and articles they had there as it had become a historical site and had quite a write up of the events that took place at that time. Angel and the children followed me as before, maybe not quite understanding the effect and significance this man had in shaping my life. On my return, I had time to look around and see what I could do in the next chapter in my life. My work was a physical one, out in the elements, in summer and winter. It was time sensitive and airlines operated on a tight schedule. I realized that I could not continue to doing this in my later years and I started to invest in my education.

SEVEN......

I spent much time and expense in the following years learning many things including property investing, flipping houses, stock market trading, currency markets among others. I was trying to both educate myself and find the one thing that would resonate with me. I had to travel within the Valley to attend these courses and came away with a good understanding of the subjects but not sure if it was for me. I did remember one of my mentors saying that we had to pay for our education. I was literally doing just that. Prince and Princess were both now in college and Angel and I continued going on vacation . For the first time in 22 years, we traveled as a couple again. It was a special time for both of us and we could see different places and move about a little differently as a twosome than when as a family of four. We missed our children, but the reality of our family was that now we would be seeing the children a little less as they grew older and began their own chapters in their young lives.

SIX......

In 2013, we invested in some property that we now had tenants in and we were looking to continue building that asset group. So, in 2015, we made a trip around the Midwest of the country visiting cities where we could possibly continue to invest in. We visited property managers, asset owners and finance companies as we tried to broaden our horizons and invest in other parts of the country. Nothing came out of this visit, but it helped us understand where the market was and our conversations with those stakeholders further broadened our understanding of the property business. We coupled this with visits to cities and states we had never been to before and made it a trip for both business and pleasure. Angel and I travelled well together and ended the trip with fresh ideas and an eager outlook.

FIVE......

As the months and years went on, a pattern soon emerged. The children were in college and both Angel and I were working full time. The search for a business or investment continued. Reading books, listening to business leaders and broadening of our minds became a habit. Our annual vacations as a couple continued and we had the delight of revisiting familiar places where I could enjoy early morning walks on the beach and Angel and I could learn or read by the pool, shop and use the vacation time to both recharge as well as take our minds off work and revisit the idea of the next chapter in our lives. At first, it did not seem as something that we urgently had to do for we still were misguided into thinking that we were still relatively young and had time on our side. So, with no timeline, no goal, no strict purpose, we relaxed and drifted into a false sense of security and the sense of urgency diminished. About the only thing I had going on consistently was that I had engaged a personal trainer and was with him for three years. He helped strengthen and tone my body and help rid it of all the bad juju that work stress had built up over the years. I took an interest in what I ate and lost weight rapidly. I was 6 feet tall and weighed 231 pounds. In a short time, I became much lighter at 205 pounds. My waist went from 40 inches to 34. This gave me an energy and a confidence I had forgotten I had before. I was delighted to give much of my clothes away as I shopped for replacements that better fit the new me.

FOUR......

In 2016, I was sent back to New Airport to be trained for a new Airplane. I spent 10 weeks there and reconnected with family and friends I had not seen in many years. I saw New Airport and old nest in a different light. I was there as a tourist. In my free time, I went about the places that I would not usually visit when I was a local. I went to all the familiar places, some new ones and as the time drew near for me to leave, I realized I was seeing places and silently saying goodbye to them. My old school, my old house, the places where I grew up in and around, where my parents, my sister and I lived. By now, my parents and Angel's parents had passed on. I realized that at my age, I would probably not be spending this much time in old nest ever again and if I returned here at all, it would be for a very short visit. I imagined coming back only when a niece or nephew had a wedding as I had done that before. I started to see more family members more urgently, met more old friends, saw more familiar places from my childhood and pretty soon, had to pack up once again, and leave old nest for home. I was happy to be going back to my family, but I did look around at old nest and wondered when I would be back again, if at all.

THREE......

Soon after returning to new nest in a field in a Valley, Angel and I went on a two-week vacation in Hawaii. As usual, it was to recuperate, refresh our minds, walk on the beach and reexamine where we were and how far off course we had become. We had attended yet another training seminar on property investment and this time, we had a follow up training seminar in Las Vegas. This was held several times a year and we decided to plan for this for the following year in October 2017. But here now in Oahu in 2016, I thought about how, in 1988, on our honeymoon, we had the first thought of buying property here in the City of Mililani. It was about 20 years old then and a fast-growing community. Located in Central Oahu it was within easy reach of most places via the H-2 highway. Given our youth, inexperience, lack of funds and knowledge, that idea remained a dream. Now 28 years later, as Angel and I revisited Mililani, I marveled at what it had become. A generation of children had grown up there and were themselves raising their families and I thought that this had all happened in the blink of an eye, but it had happened to someone else. I resolved not to let that happen again and we made preparations to seriously continue our investment journey in 2017.

· · ·

TWO......

2017 was quickly upon us. It's funny how life can be like a roll of toilet paper. The more you use it, the faster it turns. But we had aimed for the property seminar in Las Vegas in October. We started planning for it properly and aimed at combining a visit to the national parks in Arizona and Utah, attend the seminar and proceed to look for property in Florida. It would be a month long, mostly by road with flights only between the East and West coasts. We saved our money, worked extra when possible, did as much preparation and planning as we could. In 2017, research was done through the internet and the apps on our smart phones. I remember having to write letters to hotels three months beforehand and the difficulty of making bookings without a credit card. This was a while back when I was very young and poor. I had to have lots of cash upfront as deposits and carry a whole vacations' worth of Traveler's Cheques to last the trip. Now everything was done online, booked, paid for and confirmed in an instant. Angel was good with the research. Where to stay, what to do, where to go. I was good with the numbers. Flights, addresses, confirmation details, dates, costs, budget. Our whole trip was mapped out, routes planned, distances measured, hotels and cars and flights all organized in a logical, sequential manner. All we needed to do was show up, carry it out with precision, avoid snowstorms, hurricanes and most importantly, not get sick.

ONE......

Our journey started in Phoenix, AZ. It was mid-October 2017. We made our way north to Monument Valley, Four

Corners and Meteor Crater and spent time gazing at the wonders of the earth. Almost immediately, I started having trouble sleeping. I couldn't find a comfortable spot on my back and kept tossing and turning. There was no obvious position to lay in and I hardly slept. This was not a good thing since this was meant to be a driving vacation. I needed to sleep well each and every night. For some reason, I had no troubles in the daytime. I managed to stay alert and awake and enjoyed the trip immensely. The troubles only returned at night. Again, and again, I could not find a comfortable spot to lie in. Soon, in desperation, I sat in the armchair of our hotel room and slept upright in an odd fashion. Most nights I would only get an hour or two at most. I had to learn to sleep upright and usually did after a lot of hits and misses and only out of sheer exhaustion. We continued our journey to Arches National Park, the North Rim of the Grand Canyon, Antelope Canyon and Horseshoe Bend and made our way to Las Vegas. This inability to sleep properly was becoming a norm and by now, I also started to have strange sensations in my chest. Electrical currents ran up and down, running diagonally across and coming unexpectedly all through the day. These sensations were not skin deep but much deeper.

We went through the property seminar with renewed interest and then continued on to Bryce and Zion National parks. This was by now the third week and my sleeping difficulties remain unchanged, my strange sensations continued unchanged and now in this area of high altitude, I was hiking with great difficulty. I had to go slowly for I started to have difficulty in breathing. I thought at first it was the thinner air and a little less oxygen but there were older and more frail people walking faster than I was. This was beginning to really concern me but there was nothing more to do than carry on with the program. From there we spent time in Salt Lake City before taking the red eye across to Jacksonville, FL.

Our time in Florida was divided into a district off Jacksonville and then another off Tampa. We went, we saw, we spoke and came away with a clear understanding of what we needed to do next. Put up some money and get into the Florida market. We returned home with half a mind on this next task, but the most pressing issue was my health.

I saw Doctor Whiskers, our family doctor right away. I explained what I had been going through, the chest sensations and difficulty in sleeping and difficulty in breathing not only at altitude but in climbing stairs and brisk walking. He scheduled me for a series of urgent tests over the next few days and finally, I was called back to see him. His face was grave. He was not his usual jolly self and he looked exceedingly uncomfortable. It was November 22, 2017. It was 54 years after Kennedy was assassinated when Doctor Whiskers told me I had Stage 4 Lung Cancer.

LIFTOFF....

The End

ABOUT THE AUTHOR

Colin de Souza is an aircraft engineer, property investor, entrepreneur and first time author. He still works and lives with Angel and the children in Field C.

ACKNOWLEDGMENTS

The Author would like to thank Geraldine, Sean and Nicole for being the best family anyone could hope for and for supporting him throughout.

Special thanks to Mastermind members Amanda, Troy, Vicki, Darran, Ruth and Michael for challenging him to do better and giving honest feedback and terrific critique in business and in this book.

Thanks to Adam and Joe from Reliable Education, for creating a business environment that is second to none and creating a community of wonderful, likeminded, no nonsense individuals intent on raising us all to succeed. Special thanks to Adam in particular, for sharing his own experiences and providing that one, single spark that caused the author to begin writing this book.

To Mel and Wayne for running a tight Platinum program that forces us to be accountable and excel.

To Dr. Jay Polmar and his team for the terrific work on the book design.

To Mavis Okpako for tightening up the messy manuscript he gave her and turning it around in the short timeline she was given and then formatting it expertly for production.

To Owen, the first and original Mastermind. We had shared our plans, hopes and dreams and despite his own difficult challenges, has proven the ability to be free from a job and be financially sustained by his own efforts.

Finally, to his only sister Gerardine, who despite her own health issues, continues to battle on and in so doing, keeps them both motivated.

Made in the USA
Monee, IL
07 July 2026

56550192R00069